Accountability for Results

The Realities of Data-Driven Decision Making

Sandra Watkins
Donna McCaw

Rowman & Littlefield Education
Lanham, Maryland • Toronto • Plymouth, UK
2008

Published in the United States of America
by Rowman & Littlefield Education
A Division of Rowman & Littlefield Publishers, Inc.
A wholly owned subsidary of
The Rowman & Littlefield Publishing Group, Inc.
4501 Forbes Boulevard, Suite 200, Lanham, Maryland 20706
www.rowmaneducation.com

Estover Road
Plymouth PL6 7PY
United Kingdom

British Library Cataloguing in Publication Information Available

Library of Congress Cataloging-in-Publication Data

McCaw, Donna.
   Accountability for results : the realities of data-driven decision making /
Donna McCaw, Sandra Watkins.
       p. cm.
   Includes bibliographical references.
   ISBN-13: 978-1-57886-693-9 (hardcover : alk. paper)
   ISBN-10: 1-57886-693-6 (hardcover : alk. paper)
   ISBN-13: 978-1-57886-694-6 (pbk. : alk. paper)
   ISBN-10: 1-57886-694-4 (pbk. : alk. paper)
   1. Educational accountability. I. Watkins, Sandra. II. Title.
   LB2806.22.M39 2008
   379.1'58–dc22   2007026727

∞™ The paper used in this publication meets the minimum requirements of
American National Standard for Information Sciences—Permanence of Paper
for Printed Library Materials, ANSI/NISO Z39.48-1992.
Manufactured in the United States of America.

DEDICATION

We dedicate this book to six amazing individuals: first, to our best friends and spouses Jack Watkins and Mark McCaw, and also to our parents.

Jack Watkins and Mark McCaw, without your patience and love we would not be the women we are today. You truly are the "wings beneath our feet." Thanks for worrying about us and for praying for our health and well-being as we toiled through this project.

In addition, we would like to recognize two sets of outstanding role models. Our parents modeled hard work, belief in public school education, a love for this great nation, and a deep passion for learning. Sandra's parents, William and Carmen Griffiths, and Donna's parents: Hiroko Kobyashi Mettler and Donald Eugene Mettler Sr., gave us firm foundations upon which to see improvement as not an optional activity, but a continuous mandate.

CONTENTS

ACKNOWLEDGMENTS

We acknowledge the support of our department chair, Dr. Robert Hall. He allowed us to "take over" the department conference room, print thousands of pages of research, present our findings wherever we could, and gave us people support as well.

We thank our secretaries: Jerrie Walters and Karla White—you looked up material and assigned student workers to the tasks of researching materials for us. Thanks to the student workers and graduate assistants that labored hard to help us: Octavia Lee, Lindsay Bakker, Matthew O'Brien, Jennifer Bolinger, Misty Horath, Amber Otto, Brian Kennedy, and Andrew Sheeley.

We also give a big thank you to our Dean of Education, Dr. Bonnie Smith-Skripps. She would stop by our work area (at all hours of the day and night and give us a word or two of encouragement). Her interest and support are models of effective leadership.

We looked to outsider expertise to confirm that what we were reporting was sound research. For this we thank: Becky Robinson, President of the Illinois Library-Media (Library Media); Dr. Miriam Santern, Chair of Kinesiology at Western Illinois University (Physical Education and Fitness); and Jan Smith, (Consultant on Gifted Education).

Last, we thank the Illinois School Boards Association, the National School Boards Association, and the Grant Woods AEA in Cedar Rapids, Iowa, for their support, which inspired us and validated our work—we were on the right track and this information needs to be in print.

INTRODUCTION—CREATING A SENSE OF URGENCY

Education is for improving the lives of others and for leaving your community and world better than you found it.

Marian Wright Edelman

Purpose of this book: In an era when new information is being created and shared at the speed of light, where technology is growing exponentially (Jukes, 2004), and information overload is a common reality, school districts are grappling with the issues created by this fast pace of change.

This book was written to address at least three needs. First, it became apparent to us that educational leadership is struggling to keep up with the innovations and cutting-edge research in the field. Politics, and too often emotions, seem to drive the academic, fiscal, and intellectual decisions that impact the lives of countless children.

Second, for the needed changes to be made, everyone must take responsibility for the continuous improvement of our public schools. It is not enough to complain about what they are or are not. It is not enough to be satisfied, we must want more than satisfaction for our children—we must demand excellence! It is also becoming increasingly clear that funding will never match need and, thus, tough decisions about services and programs are required. This research-based book will help decision-makers confront tough choices.

Furthermore, all service providers for our children need to justify what they are doing and why. The simple act of "doing" is insufficient to achieve excellence. A passion for learning, along with monitoring and tough program accountability, will lead us to greater academic achievement. If programs are not working, they must either change toward improvement or be eliminated. High standards must be established to support higher levels of performance. Educators need to accept the reality that change is ongoing and will happen whether we are ready or not.

Districts must establish a compelling vision. The mission must be well articulated to all stakeholders. Core values must also be established and practiced on a daily basis. Educational leaders must guide local communities in the process of aligning their vision, mission, and core values against a backdrop of exponential global development.

Finally, it is reasonable to expect the data to drive decisions. It is not unreasonable for data to be reported on a routine basis to the board of education and the community regarding impact and outcomes. What is unreasonable is to continue to expect to be the greatest nation in the world with a nineteenth-century education value system. In the twenty-first century, all stakeholders have a voice and educators must begin listening to the voice. Today's community must be well-informed consumers and must ask tough questions about *accountability for results*. Accountability with high expectations is everyone's responsibility. We must all be advocates for the children of this nation!

INTRODUCTION

The American public school system is at a critical tipping point. Continuing to do what we have done or merely tweaking the system will tip our nation into the loss of global eminence. Recognizing and honoring the needs of the twenty-first-century learner by prioritizing the uniqueness of each child and establishing accountability frameworks around *high expectations* and *results* is what will tip our nation into a solid position of global leadership. A small number of people can have a major impact in creating the right culture for world-class schools within this country.

Gladwell (2000) stated that enthusiasm, passion, and accountability can effect major changes. "The name given to the dramatic moment is called the tipping point" (p. 1). For example, our nation's dropout rate should be recognized as a tipping point. To date, we have been reactionary in our responses to accountability rather than proactive. Gladwell would ask, "What can we do to deliberately start and control positive epidemics of our own" (p. 2)?

As the twenty-first century gains momentum, many in public education are faced with this new paradigm: higher academic standards and accountability for results. This necessitates new thinking from members of the community, school board members, and educators in terms of their roles, relationships, and responsibilities in the school district and in the community.

> A new interest in education by parents and community has caused educators to look more carefully at all resources and to develop an intense interest in accountability, raising test scores, collaboration among staff members, and finding new ways to connect with parents. (Johnson & Johnson, 2003, p. 180)

This thinking needs to recognize that there are diverse and opposing structures at work. Current and past leadership came from the linear, logical, one-right-answer school of thought. "What distinguishes this group from the rest of the work force is their ability to acquire and apply theoretical and analytical knowledge. . . . It gave our society its character, leadership, and its social profile" (Druckers, 1959, p. 12). Emerging patterns indicate that what will be honored in the future will be the creators, innovators, and synthesizers who are grounded in a spiritual understanding of beauty, peace, environment, and purpose (Covey, 2004; Pink, 2005). This disconnect has implications for future accountability and results.

In order to move from the present status quo toward an enlightened future, communities must begin to dialogue around some critically essential questions. Neither top-down mandates nor legislated actions will create the types of learning communities that our leadership is capable of producing. A clearly designed vision or dream for all children must be articulated. Then, a purposeful mission statement must be initiated, along with core values to which everyone is held accountable.

A common cry among educators is the lack of resources to achieve a twenty-first-century exemplary educational system. For communities to have the resources needed to develop high achieving, emotionally healthy children, priorities must be established. If we are not going to receive additional funding, then the wise and prudent expenditures of existing dollars must be pushed. As taxpayers, a higher standard of accountability must be expected. Communities have, for too long, funded educational programs with no accountability for results. Billions of dollars have been funneled into programs with minimal expectations for results. This higher level of accountability can be done through the creation of SMART goals (Specific, Measurable, Attainable, Results-oriented, and Timebound) and an accountability framework, where program evaluation is required, results are published, and actions are taken. Specific goals must be written for each building and for the district.

District school-improvement plans (DIP) function simultaneously on two equally important levels. First, they should reflect the aggregated building-level school-improvement plans (SIP). This coordinates those areas across the district that overlap between buildings, increasing efficiency and effectiveness through shared resources. An example of this might be found in a new but growing number of English-language learners (ELL). When the numbers of students are too small to receive any state or federal financial support, but academic needs are real and imperative, the district might add a DIP goal for the development and coordination of district-wide services. Second, the DIP goals must reflect the separate entity of a district. For example, the culture within some of the buildings may be viewed as good or great, while perceptions of toxicity across the district exist. The impact at the building level results in some tension, but may not be a huge obstacle to continuous improvement. Collectively across the district, however, district-level initiatives are faced with skepticism and open resistance. In this example, the DIP must address the issue of culture and trust, as a district-level SMART goal, or over time the impact will become an obstacle at the building level.

It is recommended that no more than three goals be written into the school-improvement plan. Within each of these three goals, there might be four to six objectives (actions needed to accomplish the goals). It is also recommended at the district level that SMART goals be set at one-, three-, and five-year intervals. These goals should then be monitored and reported to the board of education on a regular basis. An example of a district-level SMART goal is as follows: By June 30, 2009, 85 percent of students in grades 3–5 will demonstrate proficiency in the "meets-or-exceeds" standard on the state assessment in reading.

Building-level school-improvement plans reflect the needs of all students within the building. Some states, such as Iowa, require improvement goals in science, math, and reading. Although this is commendable, with limited resources—the most limited being time—such lofty mandates reflect a lack of understanding around the complexities of continuous improvement. An example of a building-level SMART goal might be: By June 30, 2008, 75 percent of the students at Lincoln Elementary will demonstrate proficiency in the "meets-or–exceeds" standard on the state assessment in reading.

To support the attainment of the building goals, each grade level may have a SMART objective(s). For example, by June 30, 2009, 70 percent of African American third-grade males will demonstrate proficiency in the "meets-or-exceeds" standard on the state assessment in reading. (This objective was based on data that reported grade-level functioning for the previous year—55 percent of all African American, second-grade male students at Lincoln Elementary did not "meet or exceed" in reading.)

The improvement plan is a working document. It is under constant revision by the members of the staff. The endless funding of programs or personnel with a lack of follow-up, frequent monitoring, and follow-through drains the system of financial, psychological, academic, and emotional resources. Fitzpatrick (1997) has stated, "School improvement is hard work. But if schools are not constantly improving and growing in their capacity to meet the needs of today's students, then they are losing ground and failing in their mission of service to young people" (p. 3).

IDENTIFYING THE ROOT CAUSE

One of the most common errors made in education is the misidentification of the problem. We treat symptoms, but too seldom identify the etiology of the problem. For example, student attendance is often identified as a problem. Schools will put in incentive plans to motivate students to attend. These may or may not motivate the misguided student. But the chronically truant may be missing classes for reasons other than lack of motivation, for example, "academic boredom," family needs, work schedule, legal problems, etc. In many cases, the solution is created and implemented without any input from truant students to determine if the adult hypothesis for the cause of truancy is in fact accurate. Inaccurate identification of the problem will result in an inaccurate treatment/intervention plan. Faculty and administration may spend precious time and money creating an intervention, but for the incorrect problem. After conducting several focus groups and some one-on-one conversations with chronically truant students, the faculty discovered that 86 percent (12/14) had to work to help support their families. They identified work schedules conflicting with school schedules as the reason the students missed school. Due to the emotionally draining experience of being "yelled at" or "made to feel bad" because they missed school, ten of the students had been waiting to turn the legal age for dropping out. They saw no advantages to getting a high school diploma compared to a job, but they did see the immediate increase in the size of their paycheck. What was needed for these students was not incentives but an understanding adult and a flexible schedule. Allowing these students the opportunity to take online courses, to change their class schedules to accommodate their work schedules, and/or to link these students to a small support group might increase the likelihood of regular attendance.

In the school-improvement planning process, it is *imperative* that someone asks, "What evidence do you have that brought you to that conclusion?" Until the evidence has been heard and understood, it is just a "gut feeling" or a hunch. The data represents part of the evidence needed to effectively evaluate the need, program, or idea. Data drives change. Wheatley (1992) stated, "Information informs us. Forms us" (p. 97).

Ask "why?" until there is a sense of common direction and a sense of understanding. What is your hypothesis of the problem (i.e., What is your best guess as to why your third graders do not know their multiplication facts)? You should keep asking this question until all possible reasons are explored. It is then recommended that you review your data, examine the research, and look for schools/districts that have been successful at solving the problem(s). An indicator of strong leadership is the close examination, visitation to, and replication of those schools that are making achievement happen for their learners (adults and children). Insecure leaders will not visit the school two miles away (sometimes within the same district) but will instead choose to complain about a lack of resources or about sociocultural forces over which they have little control.

Where do you begin this complex results-oriented work? There are some cautions or alerts that intelligent leadership takes note of:

Alerts

1. *Determine the priorities of the community.* Remember, the way to eat an elephant is one bite at a time. Don't bite off more than you can handle. If people spend all of their time in program-evaluation cycles, they won't get anything else done. Keep in mind that the first time through will take more effort because of the newness of the process. Remember, in the end, a formal accountability process will be your friend, not your enemy.

2. *Create a systemic process for program review in the district.* The district review should contain building-level data that are aggregated to reflect the district. In some cases, data will be reported that only reflects program-evaluation concerns related to the district. Expect that all programs will be reviewed by the board of education every three years (at minimum). Program (i.e., Title I, after school, Read 180, all new curricula and instructional initiatives, mentoring, etc.) administrators should be encouraged to conduct annual self-reviews. An excellent resource with ideas for reporting data (in addition to this book) is Lee Jenkins' *Permission to Forget: And Nine Other Root Causes of America's Frustrations with Education* and chapter 7 of Mike Schmoker's *Results Now.*

3. The American Association of School Administrators (n.d.) identified several *"danger zones"*:

   a. losing track of what's important, such as student achievement.
   b. asking the right questions *before* you start collecting and analyzing data.
   c. sticking to the data that drives decisions for improvement and not reporting data for the sake of reporting data.
   d. rushing in with too little preparation, collaboration, and focus.

4. Making a systemic commitment requires the full support of the board of education and all members of the leadership team and the teachers' association/union.
5. *Fund only those programs or initiatives with clear SMART goals.* It is appropriate and fiscally responsible that expenditures should be tied to measurable outcomes.
6. "Out with the old, in with the new," does not facilitate a healthy system unless effective succession planning is done. For example, when replacing the superintendent, interview for a leader who builds on the existing initiatives and carries existing district improvement forward, rather than starting something new.
7. Communities should not focus only on the needs of today but also on the long-term needs and improvement plans that are three to five years out.

ORGANIZATION OF THIS BOOK

This book addresses the accountability questions that communities across this country are beginning to ask their school boards, administrators, and even classroom teachers regarding financial expenditures and achievement results. Outlined in each chapter are answers to these salient questions. The format of this book allows the reader to select chapters that are pertinent to his or her district's needs. If only selected chapters are read, please be encouraged to also read chapter 18, which addresses the issue of *where to go from here.* It is our hope that the chapters in this book will give you, the reader, the impetus to investigate current policies, programs, and practices that might have gone unnoticed and unevaluated until now.

Each chapter is organized in the following manner:

a. Essential Question(s)—big questions that probe for deeper meaning and set the stage for further questioning. A good essential question is the principle component of designing inquiry-based learning.
b. Definitions—establishes a common vocabulary and understanding.
c. Research and background information to inform decision-making.

d. Reflective questions that support continuous improvement and that need to be asked and talked about within the community, district, or school.

e. Data Sets—a list of possible data that the administrative team might be supplying to the public and the board.

f. Summary—final thoughts or a summarization of the chapter's big ideas.

g. Resources for continued research and development.

ESSENTIAL QUESTIONS

Each chapter has a big question or two, around which the research and the discussion needs to focus. Johnson and Johnson (2003) stated, "The quality of an organization can be judged by the quality of the questions it chooses to answer" (p. 181). For example, here are two essential questions for this chapter:

What do we as a nation value in educating our children?

How do these values translate into an accountability system for public schools?

DEFINITIONS

Because of the complexities associated with many of the topics we have researched for this book, it was imperative that definitions be given. For example, this chapter would have the following definitions:

Aggregated data—separate sets of data gathered together to form a whole picture (for example, gathering all third-grade test scores together for reading comprehension). Aggregated data may be the quickest way to report data, but it oftentimes does not give sufficient information for decision-making. For example, the aggregated data for all third-grade state reading scores indicates that 84 percent are classified as "meeting" or "exceeding" expectations. Yet when the data are disaggregated into "meets" and "exceeds," it is obvious that the "exceeds" scores have been decreasing over time.

The district is losing (at least according to this one assessment) their advanceed learners.

Disaggregated data—data sets separated into component parts (for example, pulling all third-grade low–income, white, female reading comprehension scores on the state assessment into one data set). Disaggregation is often done to determine a focus for intervention(s).

Trend data—a trend data report reflects three to five years of data for the same report question (i.e., violence against teachers is reported for the past three to five years, not just last year or the "best year"). Decisions should be made based upon trends, not single-year results.

Data sets—data are examined from the smallest variable to district wide numbers. For example, a data set might have the reading comprehension score for third grade, free, and reduced lunch (low SES) African American males. Neither data nor data sets should be shared when there are fewer than five students within the set as this could potentially violate student rights to confidentiality. With fewer than five students, it might be possible for individuals to be identified.

Triangulation—decisions should not be made from one set of data but should represent examinations from several different perspectives. For example, when examining eighth-grade reading comprehension results, leadership might use (1) state test scores, plus (2) standardized tests scores, and (3) local assessment data to determine effective interventions. Another example might involve high school dropouts. Leadership might examine the variables of attendance, grades, standardized achievement tests, and student perception of school (survey and/or interviews) to determine student needs and possible interventions.

Research and background—*NCLB* requires that schools receiving Title I funding must select materials and programs that are research-based. Villegas (2003) reported,

Poor data systems and lax reporting requirements to date have hindered board effectiveness. This will become more of an issue now that new federal statutes emphasize the collecting and monitoring of longitudinal data for school and student performance. A comprehensive data system capable of collecting such information is particularly critical in urban districts because of their high student transience and mobility rates. To make sound decisions about improving low-performing schools, boards need accurate, high-quality data as well as training in how to interpret and use it. (p. 2)

DATA SETS THAT SHOULD OR COULD BE AVAILABLE

Some would argue that districts collect much data but underutilize what they collect. Dibble (1999) recognized that school districts collect a great deal of data and much of it is longitudinal, allowing retroactive analysis to evaluate progress. It is *not* suggested that districts and/or buildings collect all of the data sets listed within each chapter. The list identifies possibilities, not certainties. Each topic must be carefully discussed by the decision-makers and then collected. If the district and/or school had not been organized to collect the data sets, the process of collection could take an entire school year. Some possible variables that data might be aggregated and/or disaggregated by include:

- grades and grade-point averages
- attendance
- tardies, suspensions
- expulsions
- retentions
- a variety of demographic information, at-risk students
- passing/failing students
- academic credits
- students receiving awards
- results of attitude surveys (climate, culture, etc.)
- abuse and neglect referrals
- extracurricular violations
- detentions
- graduates/dropouts
- school-age parents
- student mobility
- disciplinary and law-enforcement referrals
- 504 students

- special education referrals/placed/dismissed
- use of student-assistance program groups
- test scores (norm referenced—national, criterion referenced, local assessments)
- parents attending conferences and meetings
- students receiving free and reduced hot lunches
- students involved in extracurricular activities
- conduct grades and classroom work habits from report cards

In addition, these data might also be of interest:

- students working part-time jobs
- locations (i.e., riding a bus, walking, living in different communities)
- number of teachers receiving an unsatisfactory, a satisfactory, and a superior/excellent evaluation.
- number of teachers whose classrooms demonstrated improvement
- number of classroom visits made by principals (weekly, monthly)
- number of hours/days of professional development and related outcome data
- number of parents involved in the school and the number of hours of their involvement
- number of students on medication

The challenge is determining the priorities around which questions need to be answered and which data are needed to answer the questions.

What other types of data does your district/school collect, or have access to, that would facilitate continuous improvement and the wise allocation of resources (financial, human, and technical)?

REFLECTIVE QUESTIONS

Members of your community, parents, school board members, educators, politicians, and students need to hold important conversations around the reflective questions found within each chapter. Collaboration and the involvement of *all* stakeholders—from the inception of the process—is not optional but mandatory. Leaders who attempt to operate under the twentieth-century model of "let's decide and *then* tell the public" will increasingly receive criticism and resistance. Involvement increases the likelihood of buy-in, commitment to the long-term work of improvement, and ultimately creates a better plan than one prepared by a small "power" group in isolation.

Prioritizing District/School Planning through Reflective Questions

Drucker (1971) stated, "The important element in decision making is defining the question" (p. 52). Someone must ask the following questions *before* a systemic improvement plan can be created and implemented.

What are our district's vision, mission, and core values?

What is it our district or school wants to improve?

Why do we want to improve it (giving at least two data sets of evidence)?

How specifically would making this improvement impact:

- Students?
- Teachers?
- Administrators?
- Parents?
- The community?

What steps will be followed to make this happen (i.e., desired outcomes of staff development, etc.)?

What human, technical, and financial resources will be required to accomplish the desired outcome?

How will this project be evaluated and monitored for effectiveness and data-driven results?

SUMMARY

This section pulls together some final thoughts on the topic. For example, a summary of chapter one would read as follows:

There is much that we can do to fulfill our responsibilities for providing a quality education for all children. While being cautious stewards of our existing resources, we can collaboratively create an environment where students learn and teachers prosper—where there is joy in the classrooms and laughter in the halls. Communities can no longer postpone the need for accountability. At risk is our place in the global economy and the financial well-being of our children. Their future mandates painful examination of our current practices and the establishment of high expectations for *all*.

RESOURCES

Every topic selected for this book could be its own book. Each chapter, therefore, gives some suggested materials for digging deeper into the topic. Here is an example of the resources given for this chapter:

What Works Clearinghouse is a U.S. Department of Education Web site that collects, screens, and identifies studies of effectiveness of educational interventions (programs, products, practices, and policies). http://www.whatworks.ed.gov/

The Department of Education No Child Left Behind. http://www.ed.gov/nclb/landing.jhtml

Learning Points & Associates. A guide to using data in school improvement efforts, consisting of a compilation of knowledge from data retreats and data used at LPA. Retrieved December 1, 2004, from http://www.learningpt.org/pdfs/datause/guidebook.pdf

②

PROFESSIONAL DEVELOPMENT— TRAINING THAT WORKS

Learning is what most adults will do for a living in the 21st century.

Bob Perelman

ESSENTIAL QUESTION

Why is there so little relationship between dollars spent on professional development and improved student achievement?

DEFINITION

Effective Professional Development—deepens teachers' knowledge and understanding about the teaching/learning process and the students they teach, (Darling-Hammond & McLaughlin, 1996); with a results-oriented focus on student achievement and the development of the whole child.

RESEARCH

Until recently, there was little correlation or documented evidence that the millions of dollars spent on teacher training (i.e., professional development) positively impacted student learning and achievement (Garet, Porter, Desimone, Birman, & Yoon, 2001). Schools cannot be serious about student-achievement results without a serious focus on the quality of their professional-development programs (Killion, 2002b; Sparks, 2005).

The traditional model of top-down teacher training lacked clarity of purpose, data, and teacher input and involvement (Flowers, Mertens, & Melhall, 2002); it was loosely connected to the school or district school-improvement process and was not research based. This "sit-and-get" or "one-size fits all" training model lacked relevance to daily instructional needs, wasn't motivating, lacked coaching and feedback, and was seldom related to professional growth needs (Garet, et al, 2001). Additionally, with each new administration came a new "flavor-of-the-month" training mandate, leading districts and schools on disjointed initiatives—further fragmenting an already fragile system (Fullan & Stiegelbauer, 1991). In those districts and buildings where professional development is taken seriously, the implementation fails when teachers return to their class-rooms with little or no time for practice, reflection, collaboration, and feedback (Darling-Hammond, 1998; Fullan, 1979). When the school year winds down, too many teachers find their workshop handouts on the corner of their desks or in a file folder that has never been opened. Teachers, however, desire training that reflects differentiation, active and engaged learning, and relevance to their daily instructional delivery (Garet, et al., 2001; Killion, 1999; Loucks-Horsley, Hewson, Love, & Stiles, 1998).

True costs of professional development are seldom articulated. Dis-tricts typically do not report the actual dollars invested in professional development (Hornbeck, 2003). The total cost of an all-day training is often reported in terms of the costs of the speaker(s), materials, and food. The true costs reflect the per diem of every individual in atten-dance plus the costs of the speaker(s), materials, and food. In some districts, the true costs could be more than $100,000 for an all-day train-ing. When examined through this lens, no matter the size of the district, professional development is a very expensive endeavor. Today's board and administrative teams must expect a strong connection between professional development, student learning, and continuous school im-provement.

A three-year study by the U.S. Office of Education (Porter, et al, 2000) identified significant policy and practice implications:

> Districts and schools must often choose between serving larger numbers of teachers with less focused and sustained professional development or providing higher-quality activities for fewer teachers. . . . They must decide whether to sponsor shorter, less in-depth professional development that serves a large number of teachers or support more effective, focused, and sustained professional development for a smaller number of teachers. (p. ES-10)

The ramifications of the research might be to limit the participation of teachers to those needing additional training; buildings, programs, or content areas whose data indicates a significant need(s); and/or those targeted for train-the-trainer status. This could include targeting teachers whose trend-data test scores are flat or decreasing and teachers who are not using research-based instructional practices, such as cooperative learning.

> Many districts and schools have limited capacity to translate into practice the knowledge about effective professional development. . . . professional development is most effective when it has the six features of quality . . . reform type, duration, collective participation, active learning, coherence, and content focus. (p. ES-10)

The ramifications of the research might be to analyze the data; collaboratively brainstorm questions that relate to the data; spend time reviewing the research around the questions while continuously sharing the answers and developing new questions; assess teacher knowledge and skills related to the need; and conduct a variety of types of training that are engaging, job-embedded, done over-time, and very specific to the identified need.

> Districts and schools often do not have the infrastructure to be able to manage and implement effective professional development. . . . planning that includes system alignment (e.g., the alignment of professional development with standards and assessments), funding coordination, and continuous improvement efforts significantly improve the quality of professional development activities that districts provide. (p. ES-10)

The results of the research would be the significant alignment of all human and technical resources focused on continuous quality improvement. Programs and personnel would be held to a high level of performance toward the attainment of student achievement. Continuation of programs, teaching, and services that do not result in continuous improvement should be discontinued. *Accountability for results is the new order of the day.*

The traditional decision-making model has the busy administrators planning the Professional Development (PD) for their building or district. Lambert (1998a) suggests that adults learn in a community of shared responsibility, vision, and goals. To sustain results, teachers must have input into all initiatives and their subsequent PD planning.

What Works?

The National Staff Development Council (Killion, 2002a), the National Commission on Teaching and America's Future (Darling-Hammond & McLaughlin, 1995), the National Partnership for Excellence and Accountability in Teaching, and a study completed forty years ago by the National Society for the Study of Education found the following to be effective components of a PD program:

a. Job-embedded coaching (or facilitated teacher-to-teacher learning), action research, examining student work, lesson study, demonstration and modeling, collaborative planning and development, videotape analysis, and study groups, among others.

b. Ongoing follow-up and support (by principal, department chair, coach, trainer) to facilitate the transfer of learning into routine practice.

c. Experiential, engaging teachers in concrete tasks of teaching, assessment, and observation.

d. Grounded in participants' questions, inquiry, and experimentation as well as research on effective practice.

e. Collaboration, involving shared knowledge among educators. Modeling, coaching, and collaboration on student work (Darling-Hammond, 1998; Mertens & Flowers, 2003).

f. Connected to and derived from teachers' work with their students as well as connected to examination of subject matter and teaching methods.

g. Sustained, intensive, and supported by follow-up activities. The training must be continuous and intensive with required implementation benchmarks and aligned with other reform efforts.

h. Connected to other aspects of school improvement in a coherent manner.

i. Quality feedback from administrators, peers, and supervisors.

j. Teachers need scheduled opportunities to acquire, practice, collaborate, and reflect upon new methodologies (Killion, 1999; Lieberman, 1995; Parsad, Lewis, & Farris, 2001).

k. Teachers need timely student outcome data (Killion, 2003). In addition to grades, immediate student feedback on district-level assessments are important. These data drive professional-development needs, which impact instruction and reteaching—differentiating to meet the core academic needs of each student (Garet et al., 2001).

WestEd (2003), a regional education laboratory (funded by the Department of Education) would add:

Promoting professional development includes implementing "regular inquiry and assessments about the effectiveness of instructional strategies. . . . Such inquiry may be associated with state-level reviews . . . but should not be limited to such required processes." The description explains that school leaders should help faculty engage "in a process of continuous monitoring." This process "allows for adjustments in the instructional program aimed at eliminating the achievement gaps between subgroups of students." (p. 3)

QUESTIONS FOR REFLECTION AND DISCUSSION

Evaluating your professional-development program is not only important, it is essential (Guskey, 1994; Sparks, 2005). Here are some of the questions your collaborative team should consider when planning, implementing, and evaluating the professional development for your district or school:

1. What evidence do we have that our current expenditures for professional development are making a difference in:

   • teacher knowledge?
   • teacher practice?
   • student achievement?

2. What are the expected outcomes for all professional-development?
3. What level of involvement do teachers, support staff, and administrators have in determining the professional-development needs of the district/building/individual?
4. What checks and balances exist between the expenditures and the expected outcomes?
5. What level of follow-up are administrators expected to conduct?
6. How closely linked is the formative and summative teacher and administrator evaluation systems tied to the implementation of professional development?
7. What level of follow-through are teachers and paraprofessionals expected to conduct?
8. How are the professional-development needs of the school/district determined?
9. How are the professional-development needs of the school/district tied to the school-improvement plan?
10. What baseline data has been or will be reported?
11. How much money is spent for out-of-district professional development experiences? How is the information shared with others?
12. What process exists to integrate out-of-district training across grade levels or departments?
13. What provisions are made for modeling, coaching, feedback, and teacher feedback?
14. What are the expected outcomes for all professional development?
15. What is the focus of the workshop/training evaluation form? Does it focus on content?
16. How are the professional-development offerings analyzed, reported, and used? How is the data used for future planning and improvement?

17. What level of involvement do teachers, support staff, and administrators have in determining the professional-development needs of the district/building/individual?
18. What checks and balances exist between the expenditure and the expected outcome?
19. What level of follow-up are administrators expected to conduct?
20. How closely linked is the formative and summative teacher evaluation system tied to the implementation of professional-development?

DATA SETS THAT COULD BE REPORTED

The following are examples of the types of data that might answer some of the accountability questions:

The Teacher

1. Pre- and posttesting of teacher knowledge related to the topic/practice (see appendix A).
2. Before implementation, conduct walk-throughs looking for the practice or self-reports—"Am I doing this in my classroom?"
3. Observational data by lead teachers and/or administrators of practice implementation.
4. Teacher self-reflections on their practice(s).
5. Student observations and ownership of the practice.
6. The analysis of lesson plans—using a rubric collaboratively developed by teachers and administrators.

The Instructional Leader (Principal)

7. An analysis of time spent in teacher collaboration—focused on instruction (grade-level and department meetings).
8. Are the instructional leaders in the building expected to attend all in-district or in-school training with their teachers?
9. How often is the principal or designee in every classroom looking for the implementation of the new practices?

SUMMARY

It is not disputable that teachers need training. The simple facts are that knowledge is doubling (in some fields) every eighteen months, that history books are outdated before they are even printed, and that a bachelor's degree today, in any profession, is only an entrance ticket. More time must be spent on planning the training, connecting experiences together and to the classroom, and following up. What gets measured gets done. Administrators need to submit detailed professional-development plans (including information, such as dates, times, who, what, assessment of pre-post knowledge, total costs [including attending personnel costs], follow-up plans, and program-evaluation plans for the actual implementation) to their boards of education.

School board members, superintendents, and the public at large should be invited to attend all in-district trainings. The more that everyone understands how to work with the children in their community, the better off everyone will be.

RESOURCES

Where Do We Find Time for Quality Professional Development?

McCaw, D. S., & Watkins, S. G. (2004). *Providing more time for professional development.* Retrieved August 24, 2006, from http://www.ncrel.org/sdrs/areas/issues/educatrs/profdevl/pd600.htm

Research Basis for Additional Reading

Garet, M. S., Porter, A. C., Desimone, L., Birman, B. F., & Yoon, K. S. (2001). What makes professional development effective? Results from a national sample of teachers. *American Educational Research Journal, 38*(4), 915–945.

Killion, J. (2002). *Assessing impact: Evaluating staff development.* Oxford, OH: National Staff Development Council. Retrieved March 2, 2007, from http://www.nsdc.org/library/publications/innovator/inn3-97hirsh.cfm

Killion, J. (2002). *What works in the elementary school: Results-based staff development to advance the conversations.* Oxford, OH: National Staff Development Council. Retrieved May 22, 2006, from http://www.nsdc.org/connect/projects/elwhatworks.pdf

Killion, J. (2002). *What works in the high school: Results-based staff development to advance the conversations.* Oxford, OH: National Staff Development Council. Retrieved May 22, 2006, from http://www.nsdc.org/connect/projects/hswhatworks.pdf

Alignment of NCLB and the National Staff Development Council Standards. Retrieved June 28, 2007, from http://www.nsdc.org/library/publications/jsd/hirsh273.pdf

Assessing Your Professional-Development Program

North Central Regional Education Laboratory. (2000). *Professional development: Where are you now?* Oak Brook, IL. Retrieved August 27, 2006, from http://www.ncrel.org

Assessing Your Knowledge of Professional Development

National Staff Development Council—*Tools for Schools* offers an online test for teachers and administrators to facilitate a dialogue around this important topic. Retrieved June 30, 2006, from http://www.nsdc.org/library/publications/tools/tools8-03pdiq.cfm

What's Your Professional Development IQ? The National Staff Development Council provides a free tool to assist your district in the serious conversations you might need to have around professional development. Retrieved June 28, 2007, from http://www.nsdc.org/library/basics/profdevIQ.cfm

（3）

THE LIBRARY AND THE LIBRARIAN—IS READING IMPROVEMENT REALLY ONE OF YOUR GOALS?

What a school thinks about its library is a measure of what it thinks about education.

Harold Howe, Former U.S. Commissioner of Education

ESSENTIAL QUESTION

What is the impact of a comprehensive library-media program on student learning and achievement?

DEFINITIONS

The library: The library or media center is the hub of learning in schools. It provides a place for easy access to information through a broad range of materials, books, and resources. It is structured for student collaboration and fast internet access to information.

The library program: The library provides an articulated standards-based curriculum for conducting research, accessing information skills, and synthesizing and evaluating information. Students cherish their time in a library that has a well-thought-out collection of materials, books, and resources.

The librarian—also known as the library media specialist: Credentialed, competent, and committed librarians model their love of learning and reading. They assist students in finding recreational reading materials, as well as accessing information through text and web-based processes. They teach information skills while promoting student achievement. They collaborate with teachers in the development of integrated lessons to identify up-to-date information, materials, and resources that open the doors to the world (Woolls, 2004).

RESEARCH

Over seventeen states have researched the effects of the library collection, the library/media program, and the impact of the certified librarian/media specialist on student achievement. The most recent state study was completed by Lance, Rodney, and Hamilton-Pennell in 2005 and is referred to as *The Illinois Study: Powerful Libraries Make Powerful Learners*. This study mirrored the findings of all the other state studies. The Illinois study was conducted in the fall of 2003, and 657 schools representing all grade levels, enrollment ranges, and regions participated in this voluntary survey. It included information on the library's collection and educational technology, total library expenditures, and several types of library usage. The study investigated the relationships between various dimensions of the school libraries and indicators of student achievement on the State of Illinois ISAT and PSAE assessment instruments. Higher student achievement was associated with the following:

- more hours of flexible scheduling in school libraries and higher usage
- higher levels of staffing and more weekly hours of librarian staffing
- library staff spending more time identifying materials for teachers
- larger and more current collections
- libraries' accessibility via educational technology
- school library expenditures

Keith Lance, Director of Library Research Services for the Colorado State Library Association, is one of the chief researchers in the field. He stated that the size of the library in terms of its staff and its collection are direct predictors of reading scores (Steffan, Lance, Russell, & Lietzau, 2004). He asserted that when library media predictors were maximized, reading scores tended to raise 10–18 percent. In addition, the successful library program employed a certified library media specialist that worked collaboratively with classroom teachers. The library media center was a place where students could access information resources via network access such as the library catalogue, electronic full text, licensed databases, locally mounted databases, and the Internet. A strong library media program is adequately staffed, stocked, and funded. Minimally, this means one full-time media specialist and one full-time aide. The relationship, however, is incremental, and as the staffing, collections, and funding of library media programs grow, reading scores rise.

Sinclair-Tarr and Tarr (2007) examined 4,022 California schools and found statistically significant relationships between student achievement and the school library. At the elementary level, the size of the collection, types of available technologies, the presence of a video collection, hours of operation, and an integrated curriculum proved to support improved student achievement. According to the *U.S. National Commission on Libraries and Information Science*, there are over sixty studies that have shown clear evidence of the connection between student achievement and the presence of school libraries with qualified school library media specialists. "Research has shown that students in school with good school libraries learn more, get better grades, and score higher on standardized test scores than their peers in schools without libraries" (p. 5). The Commission research report also stated that school libraries are leading the way for technology use in schools by integrating electronic resources in classrooms and throughout the curriculum. The Commission asserted that school libraries have the tools to inspire literacy in all learners and give students the opportunity to read and hear stories where they explore information that matters to them.

Chart 3.1 indicates that library-media programs that have flexible scheduling demonstrate greater student achievement and increased academic achievement in reading and writing. Charts 3.2 through 3.5 show other the correlation between an emphasis on higher-quality libraries and ISAT achievement.

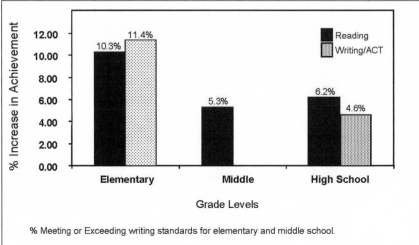

Chart 3.1. Higher Achievement Associated with More Hours of Flexible Scheduling in Illinois School Libraries, 2003.
Used with the permission of the Illinois School Library Media Association from the publication—*Illinois Study: Powerful Libraries Make Powerful Learners.*

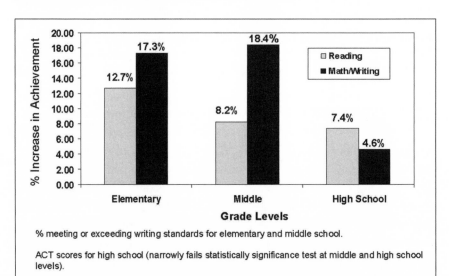

Chart 3.2. Higher Achievement Associated with Higher Staffing Levels in Illinois School Libraries, 2003.
Used with the permission of the Illinois School Library Media Association from the publication—*Illinois Study: Powerful Libraries Make Powerful Learners.*

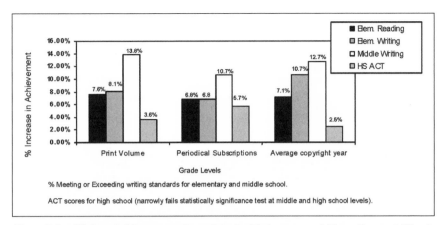

Chart 3.3. Higher Achievement Associated with Larger and More Current Illinois School Library Collections, 2003.
Used with the permission of the Illinois School Library Media Association from the publication—*Illinois Study: Powerful Libraries Make Powerful Learners.*

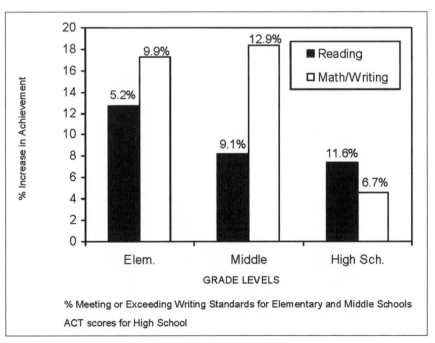

Chart 3.4. Higher Achievement Associated with Schools Spending More on Libraries.
Used with the permission of the Illinois School Library Media Association from the publication—*Illinois Study: Powerful Libraries Make Powerful Learners.*

The Illinois Standards Achievement Test (ISAT) is the state assessment. These data are evidence of the importance collaboration has in the continuous improvement framework. When the librarian provides expertise, materials, and current information around the content and the standards, it reflects in improved student achievement. This collaboration aids in the creation of a culture of collegiality and mutual respect, and connects the content in many meaningful ways. The expertise of the librarian is information access, and when integrated into the design and delivery of new information to students, everyone wins.

Superintendent Tony Marchio of Odessa, Delaware, noted that there was a direct correlation between student achievement and the services that a library performs. Desiring improved test scores, the district employed full-time, certified, library media specialists in all of the schools in the district. All of the district libraries were also opened in the summer for a reading program. The high school library has now become the community library, and test scores are impressive. The district has demonstrated "great improvement," and the district is now at the top or among the top-performing districts in reading, math, and writing. "Last

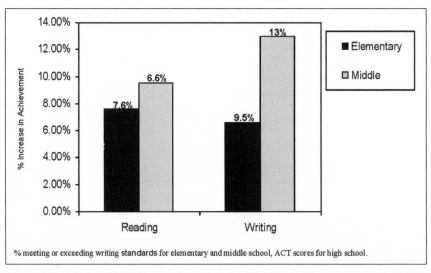

Chart 3.5. Higher ISAT Scores Associated with Illinois Elementary and Middle School Library Staff Spending More Time Identifying Materials for Teachers, 2003. Used with the permission of the Illinois School Library Media Association from the publication—*Illinois Study: Powerful Libraries Make Powerful Learners.*

spring, third and fifth grade reading ranked first in the state while eighth and tenth grade reading scores were second in the Delaware Student Testing Program" (Pascopella, 2005, p. 55).

QUESTIONS FOR REFLECTION AND DISCUSSION

1. How accessible (hours and space) is the library-media center to all students, faculty, and communities?

   - Before and after school?
   - Evenings?
   - Summers?
   - Entire school day?
   - Remote access 24/7?

2. What evidence do we have that our overall expenditures (books, software, hardware, personnel, equipment, materials, and resources) in the media centers/libraries are making a difference in student achievement?

3. What data do we have that informs us whether our expenditures for trained librarians are more effective than hired media clerks in influencing student achievement?

4. What data do we have that our current library and library staff are being utilized efficiently and effectively to benefit students and teachers?

5. How often are the written library policies and procedures reviewed and revised?

   - General policies and procedures (schedules, staffing patterns, etc.)
   - Books and materials selection process
   - Challenged materials policies
   - Internet policies

6. What equipment is essential in the delivery of effective services?

7. What educational technology is vital to the success of the delivery of library services?
8. What evidence do we have that teachers are collaborating with the library personnel in creating lesson content and/or providing materials and resources and serving on curriculum committees?
9. Is there a library/media curriculum being taught and assessed?
10. What types and how often are evaluations conducted on library personnel, and are they tied to student outcomes? Is the evaluation process specifically tied to the roles, responsibilities, and relationships of the librarian?
11. How many books are checked out by faculty and administrators? Or how much modeling is observed by students?
12. Does a professional library exist? If so, how much is it used by faculty, staff, and the community? Is it located in a place of convenient access?
13. What level of technological proficiency does the librarian demonstrate?
14. How is the position(s) of the librarian evaluated?
15. If our district or any of our buildings have a serious commitment to reading improvement, how would that be reflected in our libraries?
16. As a board member, parent, teacher, administrator, or support staff, do I model an interest in reading? If people in our community were asked which they thought the board viewed as most important—reading or sports—what would they say? Why?
17. How should we evaluate the effectiveness of the library media program?

Data Set That Could Be Reported

Monthly

_____ Number of lesson/units co-planned with classroom/content teachers?

_____ Amount of time spent on gathering resources, information, and materials to support instruction?

_____ Number of books/magazines/other resources checked out by students/teachers?

_____ Number of books/magazines/other resources checked out by community members?

_____ Number of books weeded out of circulation?

_____ Number of classes using the library?

_____ Number of lessons taught?

_____ Number of hours the library was open to students?

_____ Were any special or unique programs or services provided? If so, what? How many? How are they evaluated?

_____ How often are students using technology for research and coursework?

_____ How much time was spent demonstrating/modeling effective reading through teacher read-alouds?

_____ How many books/materials were ordered on interlibrary loan?

Annual

_____ Line-item budgeted expenditures for each building library?

_____ Staffing ratio and certifications?

_____ Expenditures over time (3–5 years)?

_____ Number of hits on the library Web page?

SUMMARY

Actions speak louder than words. What is the level of activity within your library? Many districts have eliminated certified librarians, utilizing associates/clerks, and some districts are closing the library and moving the books into classrooms. Although classroom libraries are crucial to an effective reading program, so is the need for an updated, thriving, and technologically current school library. It must be staffed by a certified librarian who views access to books as essential, demonstrates a passion for reading and knowledge, and has an aptitude toward creatively integrating materials and resources into instruction.

RESOURCES FOR CONTINUED EXPLORATION

Abram, S. (2005). *The value of libraries: Impact, normative data, and influencing funders.* Sirsi OneSource. Retrieved October 25,

2005, from http://www.imakenews.com/sirsi/e_article000396335.
cfm?x=b4TcM1g,b@rpmkgK

American Association of School Librarians—an excellent URL with many
helpful handouts for library media specialists. Some example titles include:
*10 easy leadership ideas to help school librarians become leaders on their
campuses* (http://www.lrs.org/documents/lmcstudies/10_easy_ideas.pdf) and
Collaborative Planning Organizer (http://www.lrs.org/documents/lmcstud-
ies/collab_plan_organizer.pdf).

Lance, K. C., Rodney, M. J., & Hamilton-Pennell, C. H. (2005). *Powerful
libraries make powerful learners: The Illinois study.* Illinois School Library
Media Association. Retrieved October 30, 2006, from http://www.allianceli-
brarysystem.com/illinoisstudy/The_Study.pdf and http://www.lrs.org/impact.asp

McGhee, M. W., & Jansen, B. A. (2005). *The principal's guide to a powerful
library media program.* Worthington, OH: Linworth Publishing.

Pascopella, A. (2005, January). Heart of the school: The school library is as valuable as learning how to read and compute. But it's a tough sell for administration. *District Administration, 41*(1), 54–58. Also available online at http://
www2.districtadministration.com/viewpage.aspx?pagename=toc_200501.
htm&folder=pagecachefolder

°Scholastic. (2006). *School libraries work!* Research Foundation Paper. Scholastic Library Publishing. Retrieved June 5, 2006, from http://www.scholastic.
com/librarypublishing

U.S. National Commission of Libraries and Information Science. (2004). Research Brief Winter-Threshold. Retrieved June 28, 2007, from http://www.
nclis.gov

Whelan, D. L. (2004). A golden opportunity. *School Library Journal.* Retrieved October 25, 2005, from http://www.schoollibraryjournal.com/article/
CA372997.html

° Outstanding, comprehensive, free resource (with research covering sixteen states).

4

ACADEMICALLY GIFTED AND TALENTED—OUR LOST GENERATION

Thousands of geniuses live and die undiscovered—either by themselves or by others.

Mark Twain

Once upon a time, America sheltered an Einstein, went to the moon, and gave the world the laser, the electronic computer, nylons, television, and the cure for polio. Today, we are in the process, albeit unwittingly, of abandoning this leadership role.

Leon M. Lederman, Nobel Prize winner in Physics

ESSENTIAL QUESTIONS

What resources (human, technical, and financial) are we, as a nation, investing in our best and brightest students?

Is our district providing an educational environment where gifted and talented can thrive?

DEFINITIONS

Gifted and Talented:

Public Law 91–230, section 806, known as the *Marland* Definition
(1971):
Gifted and talented children are those identified by a professionally
qualified person, who by virtue of outstanding abilities are capable of high
performance. These are children who require differentiated educational
programs and/or services beyond those normally provided by the regular
school program in order to realize their contribution to self and society.
Children capable of high performance include those with demonstrated
achievement and/or potential ability in any of the following areas:

1. general intellectual ability
2. specific academic aptitude
3. creative or productive thinking
4. leadership ability
5. visual and performing arts
6. psychomotor ability. (U.S. Department of Health, Education, and Welfare, 1971, p. 13)

The most recent definition of gifted and talented came from the *No
Child Left Behind* (Office of Elementary and Secondary Education,
2001) legislation as:

The term gifted and talented . . . means students, children, or youth who
give evidence of high achievement capability in areas such as intellectual,
creative, artistic, or leadership capacity, or in specific academic fields,
and who need services or activities not ordinarily provided by the school
in order to fully develop those capabilities. (Title IX, Part A, Section
9101(22), p. 544)

Underachievement is seen as a discrepancy between assessed potential and actual performance (Colangela & Davis, 2003). The underachievement may be short term or long term and associated with
achievement test performance and/or grades in school.

A comprehensive K-12 program for academically gifted and talented
students includes acceleration, enrichment, differentiation (which may

include grouping), and guidance and counseling. Initially, the program begins with a well-articulated philosophy, specific goals that are in alignment with the philosophy, and research-based identification instruments and assessments. Program goals should be tailored to meet the characteristics, interests, and needs of the students being served and evaluated on an annual basis.

Although a federal definition exists, it is sometimes difficult to witness evidence of its existence in classrooms across this country. According to the latest national report on the status of gifted education (O'Connell-Ross, 1993), America's top students were compared with the top students in other industrialized countries. Our students "perform poorly on international tests, are offered a less rigorous curriculum, read fewer demanding books, do less homework, and enter the work force or post secondary education less prepared" (p. 11). Finding any evidence that our nation has made progress since this report was issued as a challenge. There is also scant evidence of schools identifying and meeting the needs of those students who are gifted and talented in creative and productive thinking, the visual and performing arts, and in leadership ability.

To date, little attention in schools and districts has been paid to the achievement gap of high-ability learners when their demonstrated abilities are compared to their tested levels of achievement and school performance. The Office of Educational Research and Improvement in Washington, D.C., issued a report in 1993 entitled *National Excellence: A Case for Developing America's Talent*. The report acknowledged that there are effective programs for gifted and talented in this country, "but many are limited in scope and sequence" (p. 10). The report states, "Recent studies show that:

- Gifted and talented elementary school students have mastered from 35–50 percent of the curriculum to be offered in five basic subjects before they begin the school year.
- Most regular classroom teachers make few, if any, provisions for talented students.
- Most of the highest-achieving students in the nation included in Who's Who Among American High School Students reported that they studied less than an hour a day. This suggests they get top grades without having to work hard."

Recommendations from this report included setting challenging curriculum standards, providing more challenging opportunities to learn, increasing access to early childhood education, increasing learning opportunities for disadvantaged and minority children with outstanding talents, broadening the definition of "gifted," emphasizing teacher development, and matching world performance by taking steps to ensure that high-achieving American students compare favorably with their counterparts around the world (pp. 10–11).

In a country that believes in equal access to education as well as equity, meeting the needs of academically gifted and talented students needs to become a higher priority in America. According to many administrators and teachers, the majority of time, effort, energy, and money are now focused on bringing struggling students up to state standards to meet the requirements of *No Child Left Behind* (Office of Elementary and Secondary Education, 2001). If this is true across this country, will America be left behind in the next decade? Gifted and talented students deserve an education that develops their gifts and talents, as well as a curriculum that is differentiated and meets their characteristics, needs, readiness, learning styles, and interests. Services for gifted should be thought of on a *continuum*. Educators should be able to diagnose needs and provide the appropriate services based on the data and the characteristics and needs of each student.

RESEARCH

No Child Left Behind (NCLB) does not require the disaggregation of test data for academically gifted and talented students. However, is it not the ethical and the moral responsibility of school boards, administrators, and teachers to provide challenging curriculum content where students can thrive? Programs and services that are research-based and effectively provide for gifted students include: access to early childhood education (O'Connell-Ross, 1993), early admission to kindergarten and first grade, self-paced instruction, cluster-grouping, subject-level and grade-level acceleration, compacting or telescoping the curriculum, on-line courses, dual enrollment, credit by examination, and early entrance to middle school or high school (Colangela, Assouline, & Gross, 2004).

The research clearly supports challenging program options for gifted and talented students. Common complaints include the lack of funding to support a quality program for the academically gifted and talented student. There are several quality program initiatives that could be implemented through professional development, changing Board of Education policies, and providing technical support. These low-cost program options include differentiation of instruction, acceleration by grade level or subject matter, cluster grouping, and mentoring.

Differentiation of Instruction

Although the research is clear regarding the differentiated needs of the academically gifted and talented student, O'Connell-Ross (1993) reported that 84 percent of the activities in which gifted students were involved contained no form of curriculum differentiation. The study identified the regular classroom teacher's need for training and support when teaching gifted students. The study also reported that gifted students were heterogeneously grouped 79 percent of the time across all subject areas. These practices contradict a compelling body of research. In an observational study of instructional and curricular practices used with gifted and talented in the regular classroom by the National Research Center of Gifted and Talented (Westberg, Archambault, Dobyns, & Salvin, 1993), findings indicated that little differentiation was found in the regular classroom. The study included observations in forty-six third- and fourth-grade classrooms. Gifted and talented or high-ability students experienced no instructional or curricular differentiation in 84 percent of their instructional activities. In addition, across all five subject areas, these students received instruction in homogeneous groups only 21 percent of the time. Conclusions from this study indicated that:

- Little or no differentiation in instructional and curricular practices is provided to gifted and talented students in the regular classroom whether the school has a gifted program or not.
- The gifted and talented students in the study spent the majority of their time doing written assignments and listening to explanations or lectures.

- No significant differences in the types of questions (knowledge/comprehension vs. higher order) were found between target students across all subject areas and sites.
- Significantly more wait time was provided to target average-ability students than to target gifted students.
- Preservice and inservice training practices for teachers need to be modified to include specific strategies for meeting the needs of gifted and talented students in the regular classroom, along with the encouragement and opportunity to practice their strategies.
- The role of the gifted-education specialist should be expanded to include consultation or collaboration with classroom teachers on meeting the needs of gifted and talented students in the regular classroom. (p. 128)

What does a differentiated classroom focus on for gifted and talented students? According to Tomlinson (1999), a national authority on differentiation for the gifted and talented, "differentiation refers to the curriculum element the teacher has modified in response to learner needs" (p. 48). "In differentiated classrooms, teachers provide specific ways for each individual to learn as deeply as possible and as quickly as possible, without assuming one student's road map for learning is identical to anyone else's" (p. 2). According to Tomlinson, all students should be held to high standards. Those high standards are not the same for all students and take into account the ability, achievement, characteristics, needs, and interests of the students in the classroom. Tomlinson goes on to state that, "they [teachers] work diligently to ensure that struggling, advanced, and in-between students think and work harder than they meant to; achieve more than they thought they could; and come to believe that learning involves effort, risk, and personal triumph" (p. 2). In the differentiated classroom, focus is placed on the content, the process, and the product. Tomlinson states that the *how* of differentiation refers to student traits, student readiness, interest, and learning profile. The *why* of differentiation refers to the motivation and access to learning and the efficiency of learning (Tomlinson, 1999).

Research has informed practitioners that programs in which all ability groups followed the same curriculum have little or no effect on student achievement (Kulik, 2003). In his meta-analysis of the research on ability grouping, Kulik (1992) asserts that after "a careful re-analysis of find-ings from all the studies included in the two sets of meta-analyses, once again that higher-aptitude students benefit academically from ability grouping" (p. 60). In addition, his findings claim that there are positive benefits and that these benefits are often larger in special classes for the gifted and talented. "The larger gains are usually found in classes that are accelerated. Classes in which talented children cover four grades in three years, for example usually boot achievement levels a good deal" (p. 60). Findings from his study also indicated that enriched classes, where students have a variety of educational experiences, increased student achievement. Kulik (1992) stated that "highly talented youngsters profit greatly from work in accelerated classes." And, he also claimed that "highly talented students profit greatly from an enriched curriculum designed to broaden and deepen their learning" (p. 62).

Rogers (2003), in her meta-analysis, also concluded that ability group-ing for curriculum extensions in a pullout program produced an aca-demic effect size that is substantial (p. 65), which is reflected in general achievement, critical thinking, and creativity. Wright, Horn, and Sanders (1997) reported the results of the Tennessee Value-Added Assessment System (TVAAS) on high scoring students and found that,

> disproportionately, high scoring students were found to make somewhat lower gains than average and lower scoring students. Possible explana-tions include lack of opportunity for high-scoring students to proceed at their own pace, lack of challenging materials, lack of accelerated course offerings, and concentration of instruction on the average or below-aver-age student. This finding indicates that it cannot be assumed that higher-achieving students will "make it on their own." (p. 66)

ACCELERATION

In *A Nation Deceived: How Schools Hold Back America's Brightest Stu-dents*, Colangela, Assouline, and Gross (2004) outline eighteen types of acceleration. The broad categories include:

- Early entrance to school
- Grade skipping

- Subject matter acceleration
- Self-paced instruction
- Mentoring
- Curriculum compacting
- Advanced placement
- Early entrance to college

Even when teachers know that subject-level acceleration is the most appropriate programming option, many times they are faced with the response, "We don't do that here." There appears to be an unfounded bias toward almost all forms of acceleration at the K-8 level; all of these biases are based on the myth that the student will eventually experience social and/or emotional problems. Research over the past eighty years does not support this myth (Colangela, Assouline, & Gross, 2004; Renzulli, 1978).

Acceleration is the least-understood and practiced of the program alternatives, and it is the lowest in cost to implement. Acceleration is an excellent program option for challenging gifted and talented students. The most frequently mentioned of the acceleration tools is grade skipping or whole-grade acceleration; this option is rarely mentioned in school board policies and rarely practiced—even though a plethora of research supports this practice (Colangela, Assouline, & Gross, 2004). Early entrance to kindergarten or first grade is another form of acceleration that is well researched and has positive, long-lasting effects for student's progress. Subject-level acceleration includes evaluating the current level of performance of the gifted students and then placing the child at the appropriate grade/educational level to challenge and motivate the child for continuous progress.

ENRICHMENT

Enrichment is usually conducted in the regular classroom, resource pull-out programs, after-school programs, clubs, or Saturday school. Enrichment engages students in lessons that focus on higher-level thinking skills and processing, advanced content knowledge, and application of knowledge to real-world problems. Many times students are also involved in independent study projects. Enrichment is the most commonly practiced program option in school districts.

Popular in many districts is the Renzulli *Enrichment Triad Model*. The Triad Model consists of three components. Type I exposes students in the regular classroom to enrichment experiences and focuses on the thinking and feeling processes. According to Renzulli, Type-II training can either be in the regular classroom or in an enrichment pull-out program and focuses on the development of: "(1) creative thinking and problem solving, critical thinking an affective processes; (2) a wide variety of specific learning how-to-learn skills; (3) skills in appropriate use of advanced-level reference materials; and (4) written, oral, and visual communication skills" (Renzulli & Reis, 1997, p. 125). Type-III enrichment allows students to explore a specific topic in-depth. The student becomes a researcher and a first-hand inquirer. Renzulli and Reis (1997) assert,

> goals of Type III enrichment include providing opportunities for applying interest, knowledge, creative ideas and task commitment to a self-selected problem or area of study and acquiring advanced level of understanding of the knowledge (content) and methodology (process) that are used within particular disciplines. (p. 125)

GUIDANCE AND COUNSELING

Colangela (2005), an expert in counseling the gifted and talented, asserts that giftedness brings with it an array of intrapersonal and interpersonal issues that are unique to their giftedness. "Gifted students by their very advanced cognitive abilities and intensity of feelings deal with issues about self and others in ways that are different from those of the general population and therefore require specialized understanding" (Colangela, p. 373). He states that counseling is a necessary component in the successful development of talent and challenges schools and districts with the importance of a developmental counseling program to foster the cognitive and affective growth of gifted and talented students (Colangela, p. 385).

Carlson (2004) reported that a high percentage of counselors have minimal training in gifted and talented programming. The current counseling standards (CACREP) do not address competency in counseling the gifted and talented. This study provided evidence that counselors who reported more knowledge about gifted and talented students tended to report more frequent involvement with these students. "Finally, the findings of this study have implications for what counselor supervisors need to know about gifted and talented students in order to help their supervisees better meet the needs of the population" (p. 185).

The National Association for Gifted Children has devised Program Standards that can be accessed on the the their website: www.nagc.org. These standards can be used as a template for administrators, teachers, and parents to assess the areas of need in their current district's program. The areas of Gifted Education Programming Criterion include: Program Design, Program Administration and Management, Curriculum and Instruction, Student Identification, Professional Development, Socio-Emotional Guidance and Counseling, and Program Evaluation.

QUESTIONS FOR REFLECTION AND DISCUSSION

1. What does the trend data (state and local) tell us about our gifted and talented students?
2. What process is used in the identification of gifted and talented students? Is it research-based?
3. What criteria are used in the identification of gifted and talented students? Are they research-based?
4. At what age or grade level do we identify our gifted and talented students?
5. What evidence do we have that our gifted and talented program is making a difference in terms of academic achievement?
6. Does the district use acceleration (subject or grade level, early entrance, etc.) to capitalize on the abilities and needs of these students?
7. What support systems are in place for students who have already met the content standards and need to be grade-level or subject-area accelerated?
8. What support systems are in place for families of gifted and talented students?

9. Are teachers and administrators in our district well trained in gifted education and do they know how to meet the characteristics and learning needs of these students?
10. What provisions are made for guidance and counseling services to be provided to our gifted and talented students?
11. What enrichment opportunities are provided?
12. What are the fundamental beliefs and the district philosophy on gifted education?
13. What are the major issues facing gifted and talented students in our district?
14. Are underachieving gifted and talented students identified? What interventions are employed for these students to enable them to actualize their potential?
15. How many gifted students are identified as special education?
16. How many gifted and talented students drop out?
17. What is the district's definition of gifted and how are gifted students identified?
18. What programming options are currently offered?
19. What program evaluation has been conducted in the past three years on gifted and talented students?

DATA SETS THAT COULD BE REPORTED

In addition to those data aligned to the previous list of questions, a significant data set must be collected from building-level administrators through actual classroom observations. Administrators need to identify and tabulate the programming options and diversity of instructional strategies currently being offered.

Annually

_____ Number of students identified as talented by grade level?
_____ Number of students identified as gifted by grade level?
_____ Number of students tested who did not qualify?
_____ Number of students who qualified last year but did not qualify this year?

_____ Number of students who gain early entrance into kindergarten?

_____ Number of students who gain early entrance into first
grade?

_____ Number of students receiving Advanced Placement (A.P.)
classes?

_____ Number of students taking the A.P. test(s)?

_____ Results of A.P. testing (disaggregated by gender, grade/age,
ethnicity, socioeconomic status)?

1. Program evaluation—surveys and/or interviews of the students,
   parents, and teachers.
2. Exit interviews of graduates (senior year, five years out of high
   school, and ten years out of high school).
3. Report on the interventions, impact, and effectiveness for all
   underachieving gifted and talented students.
4. Report reviewing trend data on the state testing scores for your
   district's students who exceed expectations (i.e., "exceeds-cat-
   egory" students). (Are the trend data showing increases across
   time and grade levels in the number of students exceeding or
   scoring at the highest level of tested performance? Are data analyzed by individual students and are individual student maintain-
   ing their "exceeds" status?)

Tables 4.1 through 4.4 are possible formats for reporting data to the
superintendent, board of education, and public.

**Table 4.1. An Example of What Data to Include for ALL Grade Levels That the
District Policy Identifies Programming or Services Are to Be Provided or for
Which the District Has Available Data.**

Grade	*T = talented *G = gifted		White	AA	Latino	Asian	Indian	Special Ed	Free/ Reduced	English Sec. Lang	Under- achieving
i.e. K	T	males									
		females									
	G	males									
		females									
1st	T	males									
		females									
	G	males									
		females									

Table 4.2.   An Example of Reporting Subject and Grade-Level Acceleration by Gender and Grade Level.

Grade	*T = talented *G = gifted		Subject-Level Acceleration	Grade-Level Acceleration
i.e., K	T	males		
		females		
	G	males		
		females		
1st	T	males		
		females		
	G	males		
		females		
2nd	T	males		
		females		
	G	males		
		females		

* The gifted and talented designation is determined by the district.

Table 4.3.   Possible Categories for Reporting High School Data Sets across Gender and Grade Levels.

Grade	T = talented G = gifted		Honors Enrolled	International Baccalaureate Enrolled	Advanced Placement	Concurrent/ Dual Enrollment
9th	T	males				
		females				
	G	males				
		females				
10th	T	males				
		females				
	G	males				
		females				
11th	T	males				
		females				
	G	males				
		females				
12th	T	males				
		females				
	G	males				
		females				

Remember that the data might need to be disaggregated out in other ways. For example, how many female, American Indian, free, and reduced sixth graders qualified for either the gifted and/or talented program?

Table 4.4. Monthly Guidance and Counseling Report on Gifted and Talented Students.

By grade level	# family contacts	# student contacts	# teacher consults	# small-group sessions & average length of time per session by Topic/Need area *	Frequent Topics/ Need(s) Area	Advocacy and informational workshops**
					i.e., # of students experiencing peer pressure	
					i.e., # of students experiencing perfectionism	
					i.e., # of students experiencing "geek"	

* Topic or need area = i.e., small group on motivation, study skills, or decision-making.

** Teacher, administrator, community groups, parents, and students will receive information on the characteristics, needs, and strategies for working/living with gifted and talented children.

SUMMARY

It is not difficult to predict the ultimate fate of our nation when we are disregarding our best and brightest learners. Antiquated beliefs, such as "the smart kids will get it on their own," restrictive use of the research, and an absence of gifted policies, has ultimately resulted in many gifted and talented students being *left behind*. Teaching to the standard may be the mandate, but when the standards are mediocre and already mastered by the gifted, they do not benefit those at the very top.

It doesn't take an astronomical amount of money to provide a quality education for our gifted and talented students. For example, subject-level acceleration and cluster grouping can be implemented without new dollars. It does take open-minded policies that support differentiated instruction and acceleration. Students who are accelerated for a subject area or advanced to another grade will also need curriculum differentiation. Many times, all the school system provides are after-school, Saturday school, or outside-of-school enrichment classes. Gifted students wonder why their needs cannot be met during the school day, and they often perceive the after-school and Saturday school as punishment. Sometimes gifted and talented students perceive going to the "pull-out gifted program" as a negative opportunity because they have to complete all of the classroom work *and* the pull-out assignments. Classroom teachers require them to complete tasks that they have already mastered, sometimes for the ridiculous reason of needing "grades in the grade book."

Students are often used as tutors or teacher helpers in the classroom. The school and the teacher should ask themselves if this activity is utilizing the gift or whether we are using the gift! Decisions need to be made using current research and not from myths and fears. Districts need to offer a continuum of services just as they do for special-education students. The best and the brightest students in our school districts are special, too, and need a continuum of exemplary services offered to them as well. How can we continue to under-provide for our best and brightest students and still compete in a global economy?

RESOURCES FOR CONTINUED EXPLORATION

Archambaults, F. X., Westberg, K. L., Brown, S. W., Hallmark, B. W., Emmons, C. L., & Zhang, W. (1993). *Regular classroom practices with gifted students: Results of a national survey of classroom teachers*. Research Monograph 93102.

* Colangela, N., Assouline, S. G., & Gross, M.U.M. (2004). *A nation deceived: How schools hold back America's brightest students. Volume 1.* The Templeton National Report on Acceleration. Retrieved June 28, 2007, from http://www.education.uiowa.edu/belinblank

Colangela, N., & Davis, G. A. (Eds.) (2003). *Handbook of gifted education*. Boston: Pearson Education.

Tomlinson, C. A. (1999). *The differentiated classroom: Responding to the needs of all learners*. Alexandria, VA: Association for Supervision and Curriculum Development.

U.S. Department of Education. Free publications at http://www.ed.gov/about/ordering.jsp

*Renzulli, J. S., & Grubbins, E. J. National Research Center on the Gifted and Talented. Univesity of Connecticut. http://www.gifted.uconn.edu/nrcgt.html or 860–486–4676.

National Association for Gifted Children. http://www.nagc.org

° Excellent source.

The University of Iowa College of Education Belin-Blank Center. http://www.
   education.uiowa.edu/belinblank/links.asp
Education: Gifted and Talented Students. http://www.kidsource.com/kidsource/
   pages/ed.gifted.html
The Gifted Development Center. http://www.gifteddevelopment.com
Supporting the Emotional Needs of the Gifted. http://www.sengifted.org
Kansas Association for the Gifted, Talented & Creative. http://www.kgtc.org

EARLY CHILDHOOD EDUCATION— TOMORROW'S FUTURE TODAY

Children need models more than they need critics.

Joseph Joubert (1754–1824)

A child's mind is like a bank . . . whatever you put in, you get back in ten years, with interest.

Frederic Wertham

ESSENTIAL QUESTION

Is there a relationship between participation in early childhood programs and positive educational outcomes?

DEFINITIONS

Early Childhood Development Programs—target economically disadvantaged children and their families. Services provided typically include language development and educational services, but they may also include nutrition, parenting, adult education (including GED, employment training), socio-emotional development, hygiene, and health.

Universal Early Childhood Program—all children in the state are eligible for early childhood programs (Oklahoma, Georgia).

Preschool Education—educating two- to five-year olds through enrichment activities, social interactions, and in some cases articulated curricula. The program usually follows the local school calendar.

Day Care—supervises the care and feeding of children as young as six weeks of age; day-care facilities are open during hours that are convenient for working parents.

RESEARCH

According to Gallagher, Clifford, and Maxwell (2004), new policy initiatives at the state and federal levels have been encouraged by several factors. These factors include the sharp increase in mothers returning to the workforce, knowledge of early brain development, the number of children entering school not ready for the prescribed curriculum, and dictates for increasing student achievement.

Rothstein (2004) asserted that the childrearing practices, role modeling, and values played a significant role in achievement as well as the social and economic conditions of various classes. Children from low-income families are challenged by poorer health (vision, hearing, and oral health), lead exposure, asthma, smoking, and nutrition. Additional research studies have pointed out the importance of early language development and future success. "Literacy learning starts early and persists throughout life" (Strickland, 2002, p. 245). Children who fall behind in oral language (Juel, 1986; 1988) and vocabulary development (Hart & Risely, 1995) are more likely to struggle with reading. Research demonstrates a stark contrast between the number of words children are exposed to from the different classes of people in our society. Children of professional parents are exposed to fifty million vocabulary words by forty-eight months of age. Working-class parents expose their children to thirty million words, and children of welfare parents are exposed to twelve million vocabulary words. This often places children from the working class and the welfare class at a great disadvantage upon entering school (Hart and Risely,

1995). The implication from this research clearly informs us that when the majority of these students enter school, the achievement gap has already been established. Public school teachers, administrators, and school board members are then charged with the challenge and responsibility of closing the gaps and providing quality intervention programs.

PRESCHOOL

A recent, highly regarded research study was conducted by the National Institute for Early Education Research (Robin, Frede, & Barnett, 2006), which reported the effects of a full-day versus a half-day of preschool on early school achievement. Results indicated that even for students who are far behind upon entering preschool, they can develop vocabulary, math, and literacy skills "that approach national norms if provided extended-duration preschool (full-day) that maintains reasonable quality standards" (p. 31). This study highlighted the fact that children in the half-day program made achievement gains, but these were to a much lesser degree than full-day students. Full-day students also continued to outperform children in the control group through the spring of the first grade. The authors concluded that duration matters and extended-day preschool of good quality had dramatic and lasting effects on children's learning across a broad range of knowledge and skills.

Niles, Reynolds, and Nagasawa (2006) studied the data on 1,378 primarily African American youth who had received early childhood programming and found that these children:

- had a significantly higher level of social adjustment in school
- exhibited higher assertive social skills and demonstrated a greater ability to tolerate frustration by age 12–13
- had slightly lower acting-out behaviors, demonstrated less shyness/anxiety by ages 12–13
- had a lower rate of placement into emotional and social disturbance special-education placements.

Although no positive effect was found in the areas of task orientation or peer social skills, neither were there negative effects.

A twenty-year follow-up study was conducted (Reynolds et al., 2006) on the effects of early childhood interventions on low-income families in Chicago, Illinois. The positive findings included higher rates of school completion, higher rates of attendance in college, completion of more years of education, lower rates of felony arrests and incarcerations, and lower rates of depressive symptoms.

Karoly, Kilburn, and Cannon (2005) conducted a review and synthesis of current research and potential interventions on early childhood published by the Rand Corporation. Scientifically based research literature was synthesized regarding the short-term and long-term benefits of early interventions. The key findings were that early childhood intervention programs have been shown to yield benefits in academic achievement (pp. 65–68), behavior (pp. 70, 71), educational progression and attainment (pp. 72, 73), delinquency and crime (p. 74), and labor market success (p. 116).

KINDERGARTEN

In a WestEd policy brief (Villegas, 2005) examining the current research on full-day versus half-day kindergarten over several decades, findings indicated that full-day programs consistently seem more effective than half-day kindergarten, especially for disadvantaged students. The author concluded that a full day contributes to school readiness, leads to higher academic achievement, improves student attendance, supports literacy and language development, benefits children socially and emotionally, and decreases costs by reducing retention and remediation rates (pp. 1, 2).

Other studies on all-day kindergarten students show that they made more progress in developing social skills (Elicker & Mathur, 1997) and participated in more peer interactions (Hough & Bryde, 1996). Students in all-day kindergarten, when compared to half-day students, were more likely to approach the teacher and express fewer negative emotions, such as anger, shyness, or withdrawal (Cryan et al., 1992; Evansville-Vanderburgh School Corporation, 1988; Housden & Kam, 1992).

Clark (2002) reported positive academic benefits for all-day kindergarten. Cryan et al. (1992) found that these students were less likely to be placed into Title I, had higher scores on academic achievement tests, and were less likely to be retained. Elicker and Mathur (1997) found that all day kindergarteners had higher rates of first-grade readiness. Benefits identified to an all-day kindergartner include: increased time supported by the repetition, differentiation, and depth of instruction (Karweit, 1992; Rothenburg, 1995; Stipek et al., 1995); higher ratings in originality, independent learning, and involvement in classroom activities; less time spent in transitions (Stipek et al., 1995); and less stressed or hurried (Elicker & Mathur, 1997; Kaufman, 1997).

In the *Early Childhood Longitudinal Study, Kindergarten Class of 1998–99c* (ECLS-K), Rathborn and West (2004) reported highlights of children's gains in reading and mathematics over their first four years of school. Earlier studies on this group of children indicated that significant gains in reading and mathematics achievement were realized over the first two years of school. The first ECLS-K study indicated that public school children who attended full-day kindergarten programs had higher overall achievement at the end of the kindergarten year than half-day kindergarten students. However, findings from the most current report indicated no substantial difference at the end of the third-grade year.

What are the short-term and long-term effects of a quality preschool (full-day and half-day) program? What are the short-term and long-term effects of kindergarten (full-day and half-day) programs?

QUESTIONS FOR REFLECTION AND DISCUSSION

1. What are the vision, mission, core values, and core beliefs of the early childhood program?
2. How do we effectively meet the needs of preschool and kindergarten students?
3. What does the overall data show us regarding the expenditures for early childhood programs in the district? How does this affect short- and long-term academic achievement?
4. What data can you show us that our expenditures for all-day kindergarten are making a difference in short-term and long-term academic achievement and in social-emotional growth?

5. If you have half-day kindergarten and are contemplating implementing full-day programming, what data and evidence will you provide to show that the extended time, effort, and expenditures will enhance student achievement?

6. If you have both half-day and full-day kindergarten within your district/building, how do you compare program effectiveness related to day length?

7. What diagnostic measures are in place to ascertain the academic level of students entering kindergarten? What interventions are employed for those students who are struggling to meet standards? How do you measure the effectiveness of those interventions?

8. What type of grouping arrangement and acceleration are provided for students?

9. What does the data indicate for the four-year-old program in terms of short- and long-term academic achievement and social-emotional growth?

10. What articulations are currently in place between the four-year-old program and the kindergarten program relative to the language, social-emotional, psychomotor, and numeracy abilities and achievements of each student they served? What articulations are currently in place between the kindergarten program and the first-grade program relative to the language, social-emotional, psychomotor, and numeracy abilities and achievement of each of the students they serve?

11. Is there differentiated instruction in the four- and five-year-old programs for all of the students being served, or does the instruction involve whole group instruction for all students?

12. What promotion criteria are established? What happens to those students who achieve promotion criteria before program completion? What happens to those students who do not achieve the criteria?

13. What provisions are made for grade-level and subject-level acceleration of four- and five-year-old children?

14. How well are the actions and outcomes aligned to the vision, mission, and core values of the program?

DATA SETS THAT COULD BE REPORTED

1. Longitudinal data (following up on each student after exiting the early childhood program—until graduation)
2. Socio-emotional growth and development
3. Gain scores (pre/posttest difference) on reading readiness and language development (receptive and expressive)
4. Gain scores (pre/posttest difference) on numeracy
5. Classroom observations
6. Differentiated instruction
7. Growth in psychomotor (fine and gross motor)
8. Curricula evaluation

Annual data

9. _____ Number of parent conferences?
10. _____ Student to teacher/associate ratio?
11. _____ Screening data (number screened/number selected and serviced)?
12. _____ Number of children referred for outside services (social work, medical, mental health, etc.)?
13. _____ Number of children denied service (if program is not mandatory)?
14. _____ Results of speech and language assessments, hearing and vision screenings?
15. _____ Number of children retained?
16. _____ Number of children accelerated by grade and subject?
17. _____ Number of student-led conferences?

Haycock and Chenoweth (2005, p. 31) also suggest asking:

18. What do the birth and migration patterns look like in our community?
19. How many children are born each year to parents who are poor or have low levels of formal education?
20. How many of these children will be served by Head Start or high-quality pre-K programs staffed by college-educated teachers?

21. How can we put ourselves on a trajectory to near-universal voluntary participation?

SUMMARY

The issue of universal childcare and/or preschool needs to be resolved and districts need to begin studying the research on program effectiveness. Districts need to recognize the significant impact that early childhood education has, especially with at-risk learners. The research is also clear that it is not enough to simply offer a program but, in order to get positive results, it must be a high-quality one. Program evaluation and accountability is not suggested but should, therefore, be required.

RESOURCES FOR CONTINUED EXPLORATION

Fifth grade: Findings from the fifth grade follow-up of the early childhood longitudinal study, kindergarten class of 1998–99. National Center for Education Statistics. Retrieved January 3, 2007, from http://nces.ed.gov/pubs2006/2006038.pdf

National Institute on Early Childhood Development and Education. http://www.ed.gov/offices/OERI/ECI/index.html

National Association for the Education of Small Children. http://www.naeyc.org/

Early Childhood Research & Practice. University of Illinois. http://ecrp.uiuc.edu/index.html

Murphey, D. A., & Burns, C. E. (2002). Development of a comprehensive community assessment of school readiness. *Early Childhood Research & Practice, 4*(2). University of Illinois. Retrieved January 5, 2007, from http://ecrp.uiuc.edu/v4n2/murphey.html

Benefits, costs, and explanation of the high/scope Perry Preschool Program by Lawrence J. Schweinhart, Ph.D. Paper presented at the Meeting of the Society for Research in Child Development, Tampa, Florida, April 26, 2003.

The high/scope Perry Preschool Project by Greg Parks, Office of Juvenile Justice and Delinquency Prevention (OJJDP) Justice bulletin, October 2000.

School violence prevention: Part II, status of research-based programs, preschool ages 4 and 5. The High/Scope Educational Research Foundation's Perry Preschool Project, Ypsilanti, MI, Bonnie Benard.

Lasting benefits of preschool programs by Lawrence J. Schweinhart, Ph.D., ERIC EECE Publications—Digests, EDO-PS-94-2, January 1994, ERIC Clearinghouse on Elementary and Early Childhood Education.

ENGLISH-LANGUAGE LEARNERS/ ENGLISH AS A SECOND LANGUAGE—ARE WE SPEAKING A LANGUAGE OF SUCCESS?

The measure of success is not whether you have a tough problem, but whether it's the same problem you had last year.

John Foster Dulles

It is not enough to aim; you must hit.

Italian Proverb

ESSENTIAL QUESTION

What program-delivery system or systems will best meet the needs of our English as a second language student population?

DEFINITIONS

Bilingual—bilingual education is defined as instruction conducted through both the student's native language and English as a second language regardless of program model (Krashen, 1999).

One-way developmental bilingual—one language group being schooled through two languages (Thomas & Collier, 2002, p. 3).

50–50 One-way developmental—50 percent of instructional time is spent in the minority language and 50 percent is spent in English (Thomas & Collier, 2002).

90–10 One-way developmental—90 percent of instruction is in the minority language, gradually increasing English instruction to 50 percent (Thomas & Collier, 2002).

Two-way bilingual immersion—Christian (1996) reported the following descriptive terms: two-way maintenance bilingual education, developmental bilingual education, enrichment bilingual education, and dual-language programs. Only one language is used at a time. Language minority and English/majority learners are integrated into and taught at grade level in two languages.

Dual-language program 50–50 model—English-language learners (ELL) and English-speaking students are taught 50 percent of the time in their native language and 50 percent of the time in English. The goal is mastery (have internalized the language sufficient to cognitive academic proficiency) in both languages.

Dual-language program 90–10 model—ELL and English-speaking student are taught in their native language 90 percent of the time and 10 percent of the time in English and gradually progress to English 50 percent of the time.

Shelter English immersion/structured English immersion—English is used the majority of the time for instruction. Some of the native language may be utilized for directions.

Full-immersion program—only English is spoken.

English as a second language (ESL)—content instruction is in English (often a pull-out program).

Cognitive academic proficiency (CAP)—student is able to perform at a level commensurate with English-proficient peers in all academic areas.

Redesignation—ability to compete with English-proficient peers.

Common Acronyms

English-Language Learners (ELL)
English as a Second Language (ESL)
Limited-English Proficient (LEP)

English Learners (EL)
Language Minority Learners (LML)

Language minority students enrolled in public schools have grown exponentially in the last decade. In the year 2000, forty-seven million people over the age of five spoke a language other than English in the home. In one decade, the population grew by fifteen million individuals (U.S. Census Bureau, 2005, May 17).

The 2000 U.S. Census reported that 9,779,766—one of every six children of school age—spoke a language other than English at home. Demographers' estimate that by the year 2025, one in four children in the United States will be Hispanic (Cortez, 2006). This is not difficult to believe when one examines the growing number of diverse ethnicities found in America's public schools, even in districts where historically they have had a high numbers of ESL learners continue to struggle to determine the best way to meet students' social and academic needs.

In 1964, the U.S. Supreme Court, in *Lau v. Nichols* (Lau v. Nichols, 414 U.S. 563 (1974); Lau v. Hopp, U.S.D.C., N.D. Cal., No. C 70-627 LHB), ruled that the failure to provide special language instruction to non-English-speaking students (in this instance, a Chinese-speaking student) violated Title VI of the Civil Rights Act. Districts have a legal responsibility in the following areas:

- identification
- assessment
- adequate and appropriate instructional materials
- placements
- exit criteria
- parent and family communications *and* involvement
- ongoing monitoring of student progress
- teacher qualifications
- program evaluations

The law requires that all ELL students who are not performing at a level *equal* to their English-speaking peers must receive language-acquisition services.

Almost half of all language-minority students (4,747,763) do not yet have sufficient proficiency in English to be able to succeed academically in traditional all-English-medium classrooms. Between the school years 1991–1992 and 2001–2002, school-age students known as limited-English proficient (LEP) or English-Language Learners (ELLs) increased by 95 percent while the total U.S. school enrollment grew by 12 percent (U.S. Census Bureau, 2005).

In 2005, the census poverty rate for Latinos was at 21.8 percent or 9.4 million (U.S. Census Bureau, 2005). Poverty adds another dimension of required interventions, along with faculty training, pedagogy, and support services. Additionally, the distribution of sixteen- to twenty-four-year-old Hispanics made up 15.1 percent of that age group nationally but 38.6 percent of the drop-outs (National Center on Educational Statistics, 2001). As the world shrinks and the United States seeks to compete on a global level, the ability to understand and speak other languages will become a resource to be developed, not a problem to be dealt with (Ginsburg, 1992).

While few researchers and educators can agree upon the best program delivery system, a growing body of research has identified what must happen for ELL children to achieve. With quality programming, they can achieve oral proficiency in three to five years and academic English proficiency in four to seven years (Hakuta, Butler, & Witt, 2000). Fortunately for public education, much of what is good for English-language learners is also good for all learners (at-risk or gifted). This chapter will examine the research and will challenge districts to take a hard look at what they are doing for their students that speak little or no English when they enroll.

RESEARCH

The current research remains contradictory and controversial, with seemingly few "experts" agreeing on how to best serve ELL students. Cummins (1984), an expert in ELL, asserted that immigrant students needed an average of five to seven years to develop Cognitive Academic Proficiency (CAP) to compete with English-proficient peers. Advocates for California's Proposition 227 (which requires English learners to be taught in English and restricts bilingual instruction) proposed a one-year structured English immersion program as the most effective option for ELL students. An evaluation of Proposition 227 was mandated by the California Department of Education and then evaluated by WestEd in partnership with the American Institutes for Research. Conclusions from the five-year study indicated that there was no clear evidence to support an argument of one ELL instructional model over another (WestEd, 2004).

The study reported that less than 40 percent of the ELL students would be redesignated to fluent status after ten years. Key features that administrators found critical for success included systematic, ongoing assessment and data-driven decision-making; shared priorities and expectation in educating ELLs; school-wide focus on English-language development and standards-based instruction; and the entire staffs' capacity to address the needs of ELL students (WestEd, 2004).

Thomas and Collier (2002) reported on the importance of longitudinal data. Studies are needed that examine student performance over a longer period of time rather than just one to four years. They noted the need not only for longitudinal cohort data, but also for data articulated across grade levels. These data for all grades K-12, would give a more accurate picture of achievement data. Of equal importance, but often overlooked, is the need for achievement data from all four years of high school.

Key findings of the Collier & Thomas study (1997) yielded three predictors of academic success: (1) long-term academic instruction through a student's first language as long as possible and cognitively complex on grade-level academic instruction through the second language (English) for part of the school day; (2) utilization of current approaches (cooperative learning, thematic units, incorporating technology, fine arts, multiple intelligence, human problem solving) to teaching the academic curriculum through two languages; and (3) supportive cultural context.

Some research supports the use of graphic organizers. Teachers must remember that language and vocabulary are often a required ingredient for their successful use. Teachers must be trained with instructional tools that acknowledge, or are adapted to, the unique needs of these students. Reciprocal teaching is a strategy that research supports (Harper & Cook, 2003; Klingner & Vaughn, 1996; Palincsar & Brown, 1984).

The one thing that is commonly agreed upon by all educators and researchers is the need to develop effective accountability systems and create cultures that honor diversity. Whether these students just crossed the border or reported to school as second generation children, the data are clear—they are at a distinct disadvantage. (Gay, 2001; Greenfield, 1997; Gitlin, Buendía, Crossland, & Doumbia, 2003). Lenski et al. (2006) identified four categories of English-language learners: newly arrived students with adequate formal schooling, newly arrived students with little formal education, student exposed to two languages simultaneously, and long-term English-language learners (p. 26). These variations support the need for differentiation of programming while adding to the complexity of providing quality programming with limited resources. Schools with successful bilingual education programs demonstrated the same characteristics as effective schools that have a high number of at-risk learners.

The research reported the following characteristics of effective ELL programs:

Teachers who:

- were dedicated, highly trained, and collegial (Kirk, 2002).
- stated objectives with clear directions and examples.
- participated in systemic and ongoing quality professional development (Cohen, 1975; Genesee, 1987; Lambert & Tucker, 1972; Senesac, 2002).
- communicated high expectations (Kirk, 2002).
- used assessment to drive instruction (Hurley & Blake, 2000).
- knew how to evaluate the English-language learner (Lenski, Ehlers-Zavala, Daniel, & Sun-Irminger, 2006).
- had a high sense of efficacy in their own ability to teach, characterized by the use of two languages (60-percent English).
- gave quality content instruction in the native language and comprehensible input in English.
- incorporated the students' home and community culture into the classroom (Cummins, 1991).
- used a thematic curriculum reflecting the culture of the students (Kirk, 2002).

Schools that:

- were safe and orderly (Montecel, Cortez, & Cortez, 2002).
- have collected, analyzed, and used data for improvement plans (Montecel, Cortez, & Cortez, 2002).
- have visible and operative vision and goals (Kirk, 2002; Montecel, Cortez, & Cortez, 2002).
- have strong central office and building-level commitment to the program (Kirk, 2002).
- saw English-language learners as an integral part of the school and the school-improvement plan.
- have highly qualified teachers that implemented current research-based practices—totally committed to their students (Kirk, 2002).
- have conducted action research with all staff and teachers and were multilingual or learning a second language had student work posted everywhere (Montecel et al., 2002; Reeves, 2000).
- have provided a challenging core curriculum, with students heterogeneously grouped for instruction that fosters interaction and active engagement in learning (Kirk, 2002).
- have strong parent and community collaboration (Kirk, 2002).

ALERTS

- Educators, school board members, and other policy makers need to examine their legal requirements under Title VI of the Civil Rights Act of 1964. Lacking in too many districts are serious program-evaluation components. Is your plan of action working? What evidence do you provide to your communities that it is working? What is the process for continuous improvement of your service delivery model?
- ELL students in high school need your serious attention! Content in high school is complex (Lightbown & Spada, 1990; Spada & Lightbown, 1993; Swain, 1995) and thus requires *intentional* high-quality instruction focused on rigor and relevance.
- Integrating the ELL into an environment that honors the gift of diversity into its culture is essential. Just because ELLs and native

English-speaking students occupy the same space does not necessarily mean that relationships, conversations, and learning takes place (Harper & Platt, 1998).

- ELL students may not know how to ask questions, disagree, request help, or speak up with an opinion (Pica, 1994; Swain, 1985, 1995) and thus need teachers sensitive to these cultural differences.
- Learning second languages may not follow the same process as learning the first language. Social, emotional, and environmental variables impact second language acquisition. *One size does not fit all* ELL students anymore than any other group of students. All special-education students, for example, are not the same and are not treated thus.
- Not every child that comes to this country is literate in his or her native language. In some cases, their formal education in their home country may have been sporadic.

QUESTIONS FOR REFLECTION AND DISCUSSION

1. What are my beliefs about meeting the needs of these learners? (If you don't have any minorities in your community, is that a "good thing" or a "bad thing?")
2. What data can you show us that expenditures for ESL programs are making a difference in the academic achievement of ESL students?
3. What program delivery system appears to be most effective for our community?
4. What types of training do faculty and staff receive in working with a diverse population?
5. What opportunities exist for faculty to study in foreign countries?
6. What is the demographic breakdown for faculty and support staff proficient in the language(s) of our students?
7. Does the face of our faculty and support staff reflect the faces of our students?
8. What knowledge and skills do our faculty and staff have in terms of meeting the instructional, emotional, and cultural needs of our students?

9. What support mechanisms are in place to increase parental involvement?
10. What message does the district/school send out regarding the celebration of this diversity? (In other words, is there a sense of excitement and opportunity or a sense of "Oh my goodness, what are we going to do?")
11. What program(s) does the community offer to support acculturation of ELL families?
12. What community-wide celebrations are directly related to the cultural needs of ELL families?
13. Do classroom walk-throughs and observations by the instructional leaders report that students are doing most of the talking? (Ginsburg, 1992)

DATA SETS THAT COULD BE REPORTED (THIS IS NOT EXHAUSTIVE BUT A PLACE TO POSSIBLY START)

_____ Number and types of program models being offered within your district/building (list them)? For example, the number of 50/50 one-way programs and/or 90/10, full immersion, etc.
_____ Number of languages spoken within the district by students (list them)?
_____ Number of languages spoken within the community (list them)?
_____ Rate of transition into mainstream classrooms?
_____ Number of support teachers?
_____ Number of bilingual teachers?
_____ Number of administrators that speak a second language?
_____ Number of support staff that speak a second language?

1. Data should be reported by grade level and by cohort groups (data over time where students are tracked).
2. Data should be reported on progress using some type of oral language assessment.
3. Data should be reported annually to determine yearly growth (are students, at a minimum, making one year's growth?).

4. How long does it take in your district for students to reach proficiency? How is proficiency defined?
5. How do ELL students compare to the same types of English-speaking students?
6. How many ELL students participate in extracurricular activities?

Two levels or categories of reporting the data could be expected.

Category 1—examines the data by ethnicity, not language. For example, all Latino students are reported in table 6.1, with many very proficient in English; thus, although English is their second language, they would not be reported as needing ESL programming and/or services. An example is found in table 6.1. In this format, there is no differentiation between English-speaking and non-English-speaking Latino students.

Category 2—examines the data for ESL learners. These students are individuals who are learning English and content. They are usually given a separate examination for state testing purposes.

For both categories, data might be disaggregated in a multitude of ways. For example, one type of reporting that should be given for each ethnic group within your community and/or school might be found in table 6.2. *If* the data are not disaggregated out according to English-speaking and non-English-speaking students, data are skewed.

In table 6.2, for third-grade Spanish-speaking students, the data reported should also be examined in *trend* format—over a three- to five-year period.

The same data set should be reported for non-English speaking Latinos (table 6.3) and all other languages spoken within your school, unless there are *fewer than five students* per class and/or grade level. To abide by the Family Educational Rights and Privacy Act, data are not reported

Table 6.1. Types of Data Sets that Could be Reported.

Latino Students									
ALL GRD	# referred SPED	# serviced SPED	#parent contacts	Chronic Absenteeism	Title I	After School	Summer School	Retained	Gifted
i.e., K									
1									
2									

Table 6.2.   An Example of a Data Set for Latino—Non-English-speaking Students.

i.e., 3rd GR	Latino—Non-English-Speaking Students											
	GENDER		INCOME		GENDER		INCOME		GENDER		INCOME	
	READING				MATH				SCIENCE			
	M	F	M	F	M	F	M	F	M	F	M	F
Warning												
Does Not Meet												
Meets												
Exceeds												

Table 6.3.   An Example of a Reading Data Set for Latino Students Proficient in English.

3rd Grade	Reading: Latino (English-Speaking) Students					
	Males			Females		
	Comprehension	Vocab.	Fluency	Comprehension	Vocab.	Fluency
2004						
2005						
2006						
2007						

Table 6.4.   Discipline Referrals.

i.e., 3rd GRADE	Latino (non-English Speaking)				Latino (English Speaking)			
	GENDER		INCOME		GENDER		INCOME	
	M	F	M	F	M	F	M	F
Referrals								
Discipline Referrals ISS								
Discipline Referrals OSS								

for sample sizes of fewer than five students because it might be possible to determine the identities of the five.

Important data are needed related to student misconduct. These data are needed for all populations within the school. Table 6.4 gives a simple example of the types of data reportable. Why would it be important to compare the data from English-speaking and non-English-speaking Latino students?

SUMMARY

Research is contradictory in identifying one program/model as superior to another. However, the data reported some clear guidelines for effective instruction. Leadership must ask itself tough accountability questions related to the quality of education that these children are receiving. The quality of your ESL program is a direct reflection of your priorities and your vision. "Planning and implementing programs for linguistically diverse students requires a rethinking of the usual ways of doing business in schools" (Miramontes et al., 1997, p. 10). It is imperative that districts and/or schools complete a systemic and comprehensive program evaluation of their ELL programs. It is not sufficient, nor legal, to simply offer programs without evidence of effectiveness. This should *not* be considered *an optional activity*, but is instead a mandate required to maintain our democracy and our place at the table of international economic competitiveness.

RESOURCES FOR CONTINUED EXPLORATION

Alan L.Ginsburg, U.S. Department of Education. *Improving bilingual education programs through evaluation.* Proceedings of the Second National Research Symposium on Limited English Proficient Student Issues: Focus on Evaluation and Measurement. OBEMLA, 1992. http://www.ncela.gwu.edu/pubs/symposia/second/vol1/improving.htm#Improving
Center for Applied Linguistics. http://www.cal.org/resources/archive/index.html
National Clearinghouse for English Language Acquisition. http://www.ncela.gwu.edu
Professor Kenji Hakuta's Web site, http://faculty.ucmerced.edu/khakuta/index.html (click research).
A National Study of School Effectiveness for Language Minority Students' Long-term Academic Achievement. Center for Research on Education, Diversity & Excellence. (January 2003). http://www.crede.ucsc.edu/research/llaa/1.1_final.html
Lau v. Nichols can be found at Find Law. http://caselaw.lp.findlaw.com/scripts/getcase.pl?court=US&vol=414&invol=563

7

THE ARTS: MUSIC, VISUAL ARTS, DRAMA, AND DANCE—THE OTHER HALF OF NEEDED INGREDIENTS FOR A WHOLE PERSON

When the music of a state changes, the constitution will change too.

Daimon

ESSENTIAL QUESTION

How does involvement in the arts (music, art, and drama) impact K-12 students?

DEFINITION

The arts: a global term inclusive of visual, graphic, musical, dance, drama, choral, voice, and sculpting arts.

The twenty-first-century school district must look to preparing students for a very different future. Presently, the majority of the emphasis is placed on standardized testing, yielding many graduates who are ready for a bubble test but not the test of life. The needs of the workforce *have* changed—not *are* changing. According to many economists and futurists, including, Thomas Friedman (*The World Is Flat: Expanded Edition*, 2006), Daniel Pink (*A Whole New Mind*, 2005), and James

Canton (*The Extreme Future*, 2006), there is a need for graduates who are innovative and creative thinkers.

> The last few decades have belonged to a certain kind of person with a certain kind of mind—computer programmers who could crank code, lawyers who could craft contracts—MBAs who could crunch numbers. But the keys to the kingdom are changing hands. The future belongs to a very different kind of person with a different kind of mind—creators and empathizers, pattern recognizers, and meaning makers. These people—artists, inventors, designers, storytellers, caregivers, consolers, big picture thinkers—will now reap society's richest rewards and share its greatest joys. (Pink, 2005, p. 1)

Written in the 1994 reauthorization of *The Elementary and Secondary Education Act* is, "The Congress finds that the arts are forms of understanding and ways of knowing that are fundamentally important to education." (H.R.6, Title X, Section D, 1994). Alan Greenspan stated, "The arts develop skills and habits of mind that are important for workers in the new 'Economy of Ideas.'" The *SCANS 2000 Report* linked arts education with economic realities, asserting that young people who learn the rigors of planning and production in the arts will be valuable employees in the idea-driven workplace of the future. In addition to a governmental recognition of the importance of the arts, a 2005 Harris Poll (Americans for the Arts, 2005) reported that 93 percent of Americans revealed strong public agreement that the arts are necessary in providing a well-rounded education for children—a 2-percent increase from 2001. Yet, in many districts, the arts have been eliminated or greatly reduced, making way for increased time spent on test preparation, remediation, and No Child Left Behind (NCLB) curricular foci. Since NCLB 2001 was enacted, California (Woodworth, Gallagher, Guha, Campbell, Lopez-Torkos, & Kim, 2007) has reported a 36 percent (820,000 to 520,000) decrease in music enrollment, and 61 percent of the schools do not have a full-time art teacher.

RESEARCH ON THE ARTS

Researchers (Catterall, 1998; Johnson, 2004; Wilkins, Graham, & Parker, 2003) have substantial data connecting academic achievement and involvement in the arts. Palos-Tuley (2003) reported positive academic achievement and the degree of involvement for third-, fourth-, and fifth-grade Hispanic students in the arts. The College Board (2006) found within the subgroup of Arts and Music, the lowest scores on the SAT Critical Reading (474), Math (496), and Writing (466) were scored by students that did *not* participate in any course work or have experiences in the arts and music. SAT examined data for categories ranging from art appreciation, photography, and dance, to AP/Honors courses. In some categories, the difference between participation and none ranged from 27 to 96 points greater for those students that participated in the arts or music. Hetland (2000) conducted a meta-analysis of fifteen studies concluding that active music instruction lasting two years or less resulted in improvements in spatial-temporal reasoning.

Burton, Horowitz, and Abeles (2000) in a study that examined the artistic experience of 2,046 fourth-, fifth-, and sixth-grade students in public schools determined that the high-arts group scored well on measures of creativity, fluency, originality, elaboration, and resistance to closure. Additionally, high-arts students were stronger in their ability to express their thoughts and ideas, exercise their imaginations, take risks in their learning, were more cooperative and able to unify divergent thoughts and feelings within representational forms expressing their ideas in many different ways. Students in arts-rich schools were found to be more likely to have good rapport with their teachers, and teachers were more likely to create environments of peer collaboration, to be innovative in their teaching, and flexible in their curricula design (table 7.1).

Catterall and Waldorf (2002) reported that Chicago public school elementary students who received a program of arts integrated with an academic subject performed better on standardized tests than students who did not integrate arts with academics. Catterall (2002), in a national study of over 25,000 middle and high school students, found students highly involved in the arts performed better on standardized achievement tests than students with low involvement. He also found that the high-arts-involvement students watched fewer hours of TV, reported less boredom in school, and participated in more community-service activities. Chicago public high schools that participated in the *Chicago Arts Partnerships in Education* (CAPE) study reported ninth graders who were averaging 9.5 (ninth grade, fifth month) reading—a full grade level higher than similar students in schools that did not offer the program.

Table 7.1. Involvement in the Arts and Academic Performance.

8th Grade % in each group	High Involvement	Low Involvement
Earning mostly As and Bs in English	82.6%	67.2%
Top 2 quartiles on standardized tests	67.3%	49.6%
Dropping out by grade 10	1.4%	3.7%
Bored in school half or most of time	37.9%	45.9%

9th Grade % in each group	High Involvement	Low Involvement
Top 2 quartiles standardized tests	65.7%	47.5%
Top 2 quartiles Reading	64.7%	45.4%
Level 2 (high) Reading Proficiency	61.0%	43.5%
Top 2 quartiles History/Geography/Citizenship	62.9%	47.4%

10h Grade % in each group	High Involvement	Low Involvement
Top 2 quartiles standardized tests	57.4%	39.3%
Top 2 quartiles Reading	56.5%	37.7%
Level 2 (high) Reading Proficiency	58.8%	42.9%
Top 2 quartiles History/Geography/Citizenship	54.6%	39.7%

Catterall, Chapleau, and Iwanaga's study (as cited in Deasy, 2002a, p. 6).

Research has found that curriculum in the arts helps students develop imagination (Greene, 1995), motivation to learn (Csikszentmihalyi, 1997), creativity, social skills (Catterall, 1998; Harland, et al., 2000), and lower dropout rates. Current brain research shows a strong connection between a high-quality arts program and academic achievement. Schools that precipitously cut music and art are creating an environment void of the opportunity to develop the creative side of the brain.

Vaughn (2002) found that students who took music classes in high school were more likely to score higher on standardized math tests, such as the SAT. Catterall, Chapleau, and Iwanaga (2002) reported that middle and high school students consistently involved in band or orchestra performed better in senior-year math. The results were even more impressive for low-income students involved in band or orchestra; they scored twice the score of their artistically uninvolved peers. The National Association of State Boards of Education (Meyer, 2005) investigated the status of our nation's arts curricula. The study group supported the research-basis for arts in our schools and reported concern over the marginalization of the arts that has occurred. Their report identified the arts curricula as the "lost curriculum" (p. 35).

Teachers reported that having an arts curriculum positively influenced the students (Upitis & Smithrim, 2003):

- 31 percent said the curriculum engaged students and motivated them to learn.
- 15 percent said feelings of success were fostered in most students.
- 15 percent said that it allowed for a variety of learning styles.

Upitis and Smithrim (2003) found that students, teachers, and administrators reported that a Learning Through the Arts (LTTA) curriculum made students more involved in learning. Students particularly mentioned desiring more physical activity in their daily curriculum. Seventy-seven percent of LTTA sixth-grade boys did well or very well in school, compared to 73 percent of sixth-grade boys in other schools, but this was not significant. While 43.8 percent of low socioeconomic status (SES) students who were highly involved in the arts scored in the top two quartiles in reading (Catterall, Chapleau, & Iwanaga, 2005). Harland et al. (2000) also reported a positive effect on the culture of the school.

LTTA schools in Canada found that (Upitis & Smithrim, 2003) students in sixth-grade classes performed no better in reading than those in other schools, but their scores were higher in mathematics (scores in geometry and applications of mathematical concepts). Writing scores were higher than those in other schools, and female students reported feeling happier and voiced a stronger desire to attend school. Highly involved arts students were:

- 4 times more likely to be recognized for academic achievement.
- 3 times more likely to be elected to class office within their schools.
- 4 times more likely to participate in a math and science fair.
- 3 times more likely to win an award for school attendance.
- 4 times more likely to win an award for writing an essay or poem.

What can school boards and school administrators do to support the arts? According to the American for the Arts (2005) they can:

- establish a district-wide education policy that identifies and funds the arts as a key component in a complete education;
- allocate a percentage of the district's general operating budget to arts education programming;
- foster partnerships with local and state arts agencies and cultural institutions in an effort to broaden support and resources; and
- be an informed advocate for arts education within the community. (para. 2)

Drama nurtures empathy and the valuing of others (Harland et al., 2000), but it is lacking in status in the school curriculum. Catterall's study (as cited in Deasy, 2002b) found that dramatic conversations gave students the opportunity to experiment with expression and communication. Catterall's review of the literature on drama found kindergarten through third grade as the primary population for study. The research shows strong connections between dramatic enactment and reading comprehension, oral story understanding, and written story understanding. Studies focused on older students found drama impacted reading skills, persuasive and narrative writing ability, and children's self-conceptions as readers and learners. Walsh-Bowers (1992) reported the impact of a creative drama program focused on transitioning students from middle/junior high into high school. The program also reported strengthened peer relationships.

FINE ARTS QUESTIONS FOR CONTINUOUS IMPROVEMENT, DIALOGUE, AND POSSIBLE DATA SETS: DRAMA, PUBLIC SPEAKING, DEBATE, GRAPHIC AND VISUAL ARTS

1. What is currently being done within our district to foster the development of creativity?
2. How committed are we to the development of balanced and/or well-rounded citizens of the future? If we are committed, what evidence could we provide that supports the development of both the right and left hemispheres of the child?
3. What is the level of access to the fine arts?

4. What is the local relationship between the fine arts and the curricula?
5. How aligned to the standards is the fine arts curricula?
6. What assessments are given and how frequently are those data reported?
7. What, if any, correlation or relationship does the data for fine arts have to other assessment data collected (for example, by grade level, standards, building, fine arts teacher, individual student)?

   a. Is there any predictability between student performance on any fine arts assessment(s) and/or any academic assessments? These data sets will require comparisons using trend data. It cannot be done with less than three years of data to compare.
   b. What, if any, correlation or relationship can be reported for subgroups:

      i.   Gender?
      ii. Grade/age?
      iii. Ethnicity?
      iv. Income?
      v.   Ability/achievement levels?

8. How are the fine arts integrated into the curricula? Are there coordinated efforts to integrate music and art into social sciences, history, English, and physical education curriculum?
9. How often are the written curricula and outcomes reviewed and evaluated?
10. How is technology integrated into the instructional design of the fine arts curricula?
11. What opportunities for performance, public demonstrations, and/or exhibits exist for students and/or faculty/staff?
12. What opportunities for music composition exist?
13. How involved/engaged is the community with your fine arts program?
14. What is currently being offered by the music specialists, classroom teachers, and community?

15. What is the budget for the fine arts within your district and for each building?

16. When is the program-evaluation report shared with the community and/or the board of education?

   a. How often are parents and students allowed input into the arts program regarding:

      i.   Program effectiveness?
      ii. Program impact?
      iii. Responses to individual creativity?
      iv. Program design and implementation?

17. Competition is not necessarily a vital component of a quality arts program, but it is often included. If your district/school has competition as a part of its design:
   a. Does everyone get to participate? If not, why not?
   b. Is competition limited to certain program areas (such as music) and not supported for other artistic areas? Are sufficient resources allocated for the equal support of all opportunities for competition?

18. How are the educators evaluated? Is the same instrument used for evaluating your fine arts teaching staff as your core academics?

19. How is professional development evaluated and shared? What types of professional-development opportunities are offered? Are they specific to the continued development of the teachers' artistic knowledge, skills, and pedagogical development? Does training focus on effective integration of the arts into the entire curricula? If so, what level of follow-up exists and how is it reported?

20. What opportunities for articulation across grade levels of a cogent curricula development are given? Are grade levels or programs (by reputation) recognized as being stronger? Why? How effectively are you duplicating those programs or program variables? (No student, grade level, or building deserves less than another just because of personalities, collective bargaining agreements, or budgets.)

DATA SETS THAT COULD BE REPORTED

1. How many minutes of instruction do students at each grade receive in:

   a. Graphic/visual arts?
   b. Music?

       i. Instrumental?
       ii. Choral?

   c. Dance?
   d. Drama?
   e. Speech and Debate?

2. How many performances and/or public exhibits are completed? What are the outcomes, if there are any to report (for example, what is the total number of superior blue ribbons at the state music competition by grade, gender, income, race)?
3. How do you track students (by demographic data such as gender, ethnicity, gifted, income, special education, and other variables as determined important for your community) participating in each of the arts program offered by your district/school?
4. How do students participating in the arts perform academically?
5. How many classes integrate the arts into their curriculum? How often? How is this assessed?
6. What extended learning and/or outside opportunities for participation in the arts?
7. What is the annual budget for the arts?
8. How many students are identified as talented in the arts? How many services and/or programs are offered to meet their needs? (These do not need to be the sole responsibility of the school/district, but they do need to be reported.)

SUMMARY

The National Art Education Association reported (as cited in Chapman, 2004) that 25 percent of principals had cut arts education and 33 percent anticipated future reductions. The research clearly supports the academic benefits of a strong arts program for all children, especially those at risk of academic failure. As a community, we cannot claim to value the uniqueness of each child and not recognize that many children thrive in an environment rich in the arts. The issue of access and equity also needs to be addressed. The probability of being involved in the arts was much higher for students with higher socioeconomic status (Caterall, Chapleau & Iwanaga, 2005) than for children of poverty; this must be changed *if* no child is truly to be left behind.

RESOURCES FOR CONTINUED EXPLORATION

Music in Our Schools Month

National Association for Music Education (http://www.menc.org) communicates the importance of music in the learning experience of all students.

Youth Art Month

Council for Art Education (http://www.acminet.org/) emphasizes the importance of art activities and encourages schools and youth groups to support their art programs.

Community Arts Education Project

Sponsored by California PTA and California Alliance for Arts Education (http://www.artsed411.org/projects/caep.stm), the community Arts Education Project gives an excellent example of an audit and audit report that an art department could modify for reporting to their public and board of education.

National Endowment for the Arts

The National Endowment for the Arts is dedicated to supporting excellence in the arts, both new and established programs. The agency provides leadership in arts education. The Endowment is the nation's largest funder of the arts and brings art to all 50 states, including rural areas, inner cities, and military bases.

8

PHYSICAL EDUCATION AND STUDENT WELLNESS—AS STRONG AS OUR WEAKEST LINK

Physical fitness is not only one of the most important keys to a healthy body, it is the basis of dynamic and creative intellectual activity.

John Fitzgerald Kennedy

ESSENTIAL QUESTION

How effectively are the services being provided and evaluated that support health, and fitness?

DEFINITIONS

Physical education—Physical education is a planned instructional program with specific objectives. As an essential part of the total curriculum, physical education programs increase physical competence, health-related fitness, self-responsibility, and enjoyment of physical activity for all students so that they can establish physical activity as a natural part of everyday life (National Association for Sport and Physical Education, 2006, p. 8).

Wellness—an active process of becoming aware of and making choices toward a more successful existence (National Wellness Association, n.d., para. 1).

RESEARCH

Physical education is on the public radar screen. The prevalence of overweight children in the U.S. has nearly tripled since 1980 (Hedley et al., 2004) while approximately 10 percent of children ages two to five are overweight (Ogden, Flegal, Carroll, & Johnson, 2002). "The CDC reported that nearly one-third of elementary schools nationwide no longer offer recess, and, between 1991 and 2003, the number of high school students taking PE declined from 41 percent to 28 percent" (Schibsted, 2006, p. 8). In total, about 25 million U.S. children and adolescents are overweight or nearly overweight (Mayo Clinic, n.d.). The National Association for Sport and Physical Education recommends that children get a minimum of sixty minutes per day of combined moderate and vigorous physical activity. In 2003, only one-third of high school students met this standard. A study by the California Department of Education (2001) found a relationship between physical fitness and academic achievement.

- Higher achievement was correlated with higher test scores on the SAT-9 at fifth, seventh, and ninth grade.
- The relationship was stronger in math than in reading.
- Students who met the minimum fitness requirements in three or more areas showed the greatest achievement gains in fifth, seventh, and ninth grade.
- Females had higher achievement than males, particularly when they also had high fitness levels.

The impact of obesity on society through increased morbidity, mortality, and cost of medical care has been reported by the Center for Disease Control and Prevention as significant. According to *The Surgeon General's Call to Action to Prevent and Decrease Overweight and Obesity* (U.S. Department of Health and Human Services, 2001), the cost of obesity in the United States in 2000 was more than $117 billion ($61 billion direct and $56 billion indirect). Among children and adolescents, overweight or obesity is linked to emotional and social problems and to serious medical conditions, such as Type 2 diabetes, hypertension, dyslipidemia, depression, metabolic syndrome, asthma and other respiratory problems, sleep disorders, liver disease, early puberty or menarche, eating disorders, and skin infections (Mayo Clinic, n.d.).

As childhood obesity continues to skyrocket in this country, the need for quality physical education programs is greater than ever. There are no federal regulations requiring physical education or fitness (National Association for Sport and Physical Education, 2006), and the state requirements vary greatly. Twelve states allow students to fulfill physical education credits (required for graduation) through online courses (National Association for Sport and Physical Education, 2006).

Arkansas has responded to the obesity problem with legislation mandating annual statewide body mass index (BMI) assessments of all public school students. Results reported that, during the 2003–2004 and 2004–2005 school years, 38 percent of Arkansas students were overweight or at risk for obesity. California and Illinois also require body mass indexing at the fifth and ninth grades (National Association for Sport and Physical Education, 2006). However, assessment alone does not solve the problem.

Little accountability related to the outcomes for physical education exists. As childhood obesity continues to skyrocket in this country, the need for quality physical education programs is greater than ever. The connections between fitness and academic achievement have been documented. Around 200 studies demonstrate the relationship between physical education or fitness and academic achievement (Etnier, Salazar, Landers, Petruzzello, Han, & Nowell, 1997). Physical activity programs are linked to higher achievement (Etnier et al., 1997) and increased concentration and has improved writing, reading, and math test scores (Symons, Cinelli, James, & Groff, 1997). Providing more time for physical education has been linked to higher test scores, especially in mathematics (Shephard, 1997). Students who have P.E. classes every day have better attitudes about school, attendance, and academic achievement (National Association for Sport and Physical Education, 2001). Seventy-two percent of student leaders say schools should make P.E. a priority, and 81 percent say more students need to get involved in physical activity (Action for Healthy Kids, 2002).

Wellness

Section 204 of the Child Nutrition Act (2004) requires that all schools receiving federal reimbursement for school lunch or breakfast programs must have a local wellness policy in place by 2006–2007. Policy development must be completed by a comprehensive group of stakeholders (students, parents, public, food services personnel, administrators, and board members). At a minimum, these policies must include nutrition education and guidelines, physical activity goals, and a program-evaluation component—assessing the effectiveness of the implementation of the policy. The overall improvement of the health and well-being of our children is not simply a school's concern but also a community issue. It is therefore imperative that the community focus their limited resources of time, energy, and funding into a unified program of assessment and initiatives. It is also important that student voices be heard during the development of all wellness programs. The overall development of healthy children is no longer optional; it now requires a strong sense of urgency, focus, and commitment. As communities, we need to "walk the talk" in more ways than one.

QUESTIONS FOR REFLECTION AND DISCUSSION

1. What is the overall physical condition of our students?
2. How much modeling of healthy living do students and community members witness from the board of education, administrators, support staff, and faculty?
3. How well articulated is the PK-12 physical education curriculum?
4. How is fitness assessed and reported?
5. What results can be provided that substantiate the effectiveness of our physical education program(s)?
6. What assessments are tied to the written physical education curriculum?
7. How are outcomes reported to students and parents?
8. Is physical fitness a part of the overall culture of your district and/or school?
9. How much time and energy is committed to the health curriculum?

10. Are all of the physical education teachers certified in physical education and health? Do they model physical fitness?

11. Do all physical educators stay current in their knowledge and skills by belonging to and being active in the state and national associations (i.e., National Association for Sport and Physical Education [NASPE])?

12. How is fitness (for all students) celebrated in your community, district, and/or school?

13. Is there a wellness policy (as mandated by law)? Is the policy monitored and used? What evidence could be provided that it is being used?

14. How are physical educators evaluated? Are there specific and different criteria within the evaluation form that examine the implementation of the physical education curriculum, assessments, and the creation and implementation of fitness and wellness activities for the school and/or community?

15. What data do we have that our expenditures for student support personnel are making a difference in the attitudes, behaviors, and the achievements of our students in PK-12?

DATA SETS THAT COULD BE REPORTED FOR PHYSICAL EDUCATION

1. How many students achieved a ranking of Does Not Meet, Meets, and Exceeds (by gender, grade level, and ethnicity) on the district fitness and/or wellness assessment?

2. What is the physical fitness status of the adults (board of education, administrators, teachers, and support staff) within the district?

3. How many adults participated in the district fitness programs?

4. How many minutes per week is each grade level required to participate in physical education?

5. How many students each quarter are exempted from physical education class? Why?

6. How much money is allocated to the health curriculum?

7. What grade levels receive instruction in health? Is the health curriculum a "stand alone" content area or is it integrated into other

areas? If it is integrated, what evidence can be provided that the content is not lost or minimized? For example, is the integration of the health curricula content at a superficial level (i.e., so we can say we have "covered" the material) or a level of integrity?

8. How often does the district have a discussion around total fitness that involves the following (at a minimum): nursing, school psychologists, school social worker, speech therapists, physical educators, health educators, food service, and administration?

9. How is your school lunch program evaluated? (Does your school follow the Department of Agriculture standard?) How student-friendly are the menu selections? Are fruit and salads daily options?

10. How much money is allocated to specific sports programs?

SUMMARY OF STUDENT WELLNESS AND PHYSICAL EDUCATION

What is there to gain when the United States commands first place in the global science, math, and technology race if our children are overweight, physically ill, emotionally maladjusted (unhappy, depressed, suicidal, selfish, mean-spirited), and not centered, maturing individuals? Attention must not be solely focused on test scores. Modeling wellness and expecting overall well-being for our children should be a national priority.

RESOURCES FOR CONTINUED EXPLORATION

The National Association for Sport and Physical Education has a web page template for local school wellness policies (http://www.aahperd.org/naspe/template.cfm?template=wellness.html).

The National School Boards Association—School Health Programs. http://www.nsba.org/site/page_SH_home.asp?TRACKID=&VID=62&CID=1113&DID=12019

If you are interested in your state's physical education program status download and read: 2006 *Shape of a Nation Report: Status of Physical Education in the USA.* http://www.aahperd.org/NASPE/ShapeOfTheNation/PDF/ShapeOfTheNation.pdf

Calculate your body mass index (BMI) at http://www.caloriecontrol.org/bmi. html

Action for Healthy Kids—an online tool that will assist a district in the development of their wellness policy (http://www.actionforhealthykids.org/).

After-school programs that fight obesity with nutrition & exercise. http://www. ccscenter.org/images/library/File/afterschool/Exemplary%20Practices.pdf

9

STUDENT SUPPORT SERVICES: PERSONNEL AND PROGRAMS—ONE PART INTELLECTUAL, TWO PARTS SOCIAL AND EMOTIONAL

Be alert to give service. What counts a great deal in life is what we do for others.

Anonymous

Try not to become a man of success but rather try to become a man of value.

Albert Einstein

ESSENTIAL QUESTION

How effectively are the student support services helping students to be healthy, adjusted, and engaged learners?

DEFINITIONS

The following definitions are embedded within each professional field being researched.

RESEARCH

Accountability for results is relatively new to some of the student support services. Some would say that they have been too busy doing their work to do the research; others would say that they should have been doing both. In researching these support areas, national associations (such as the National Association of School Social Workers and the National Association of School Nurses) have recognized the urgent need for their members to produce results that are directly connected to student achievement.

> Everyone knows the importance of having data on **results**. Few would argue against being **accountable** for their actions and outcomes. But solving complex problems requires use of comprehensive, multifaceted, and integrated interventions, and thus, the accountability framework also must be comprehensive, multifaceted, and integrated. (U.C.L.A. Center for Mental Health in Schools, 2000, para. 1)

In some cases, the evidence is difficult to acquire. It is difficult to prove prevention. For example, it is somewhat difficult to provide evidence of what you have prevented from happening, such as suicide, drug use, or teen pregnancy. Boards, administrators, and the community often react only when tragedy strikes, not when it is prevented. Even though documentation of impact is difficult to produce, student support personnel need to attempt to do so. School nurses, guidance counselors, school psychologists, and social workers play an important role in the overall well-being of our students. The U.S. Department of Education: Special Education and Rehabilitative Services *Early Warning—Timely Response* report identified warning signs for school violence that can help frame concern for a child. They warned:

> Teachers and administrators and other school support staff are not professionally trained to analyze children's feelings and motives. But they are on the front line when it comes to observing troublesome behavior and making referrals to appropriate professionals, such as school psychologists, social workers, counselors, and nurses. (p. 6)

There is recognition of the important role that student support services provide during these volatile and difficult times of school safety.

Yet, more must be done to document their contribution to the academic, emotional, and psychological development of our children.

School nurses are more involved every year as schools see an increase in the number of allergies, asthma, ear problems, vision problems, and, more recently, the childhood obesity problem. School counselors are in the majority of high schools in this country and provide the needed services of vocational guidance, testing and assessment, interviewing, small-group and individual counseling, along with classroom guidance, counseling, and study skills groups. They are also heavily involved in parent conferences and referrals to community agencies. Some states, but not all, have mandated guidance and counseling programs PK-12. Although administrators and teachers recognize the growing emotional and psychological needs of their students, resource allocations in many districts limit the availability of these positions.

School social workers play an important role in linking the school to families. Any family may become at risk due to illness, death, unemployment, or other personally challenging circumstances. School psychologists are employed to evaluate socio-emotional, intellectual, and academic problems that interfere with students' learning. Additionally, they often make recommendations for classroom interventions, as well as services and internal and external referrals. School psychologists meet with classroom teachers in a consultative role to assist with students who have behavioral and or emotional problems as well as academic and learning problems. They meet with parents and teachers to help assess the needs of the child and to make recommendations that will enhance the academic and social–emotional well-being of the student.

Research on School Nurses

For learning to take place, attendance (either physically or virtually) is a minimum requirement. Chronic health issues are on the rise, whether it is the increased number of allergies (food, medications, insects, environmental), diabetes mellitus, obesity, physical disabilities, HIV/AIDS, or asthma.

The *Scope and Standards of Professional School Nursing Practice* (Selekman & Guilday, 2003) states that school nurses should evaluate the quality and effectiveness of their practice. The association identified ten outcome-based areas:

(a) increased student seat time, (b) receipt of first aid and acute care measures, (c) receipt of competent health-related interventions or skills, (d) meeting of the comprehensive needs of children with chronic conditions, (e) enhanced school health via wellness promotion and disease prevention measures, (f) referrals, (g) safe environment, (h) enhanced school health via community outreach, (i) cost-effective school nurse services, and (j) student, parent, and staff satisfaction. (p. 344)

For those students with chronic health problems (AIDS, diabetes, allergies, etc.), the presence of an effective school nurse and counselor facilitated not only their attendance but also provided a necessary advocacy voice with teachers, administrators, and other students (Jones, 2006).

The *American Lung Association* (2006) estimated 6.2 million U.S. children under the age of eighteen suffer from asthma, while the Centers for Disease Control (2004) estimates 9 million. Four million students suffered an asthmatic attack or episode in 2004. The fatality rates in 2003 were more than 4,099 deaths. Asthma is the third leading cause of hospitalization for children under the age of fifteen. In 2004, asthma accounted for approximately fourteen million lost attendance days for school-age children. It was the number one cause of student absenteeism related to chronic medical conditions. Taras (2004) found that students with asthma were absent about one day more than those without asthma. This study examined the use of a school nurse as a case manager for students with asthma. School nurses taught the Open Airways for Schools program, which include educational interventions to improve knowledge and self-management skills, grades, and asthma morbidity. There was no relationship between the case-management program and absenteeism. Students who had a case manager were more likely to have an inhaler at school ($N = 60.7$) and use a peak flow meter ($N = 23.8$) when compared to those without a case manager ($N = 34.3$, $N = 5.8$).

In addition to student achievement, attendance, emotional support, and health education as reasons for the presence of an effective school nurse, it is also the nurse's responsibility to dispense medications. One study of the nurse-to-student ratio found that:

- Districts with more nurses per student (low ratios) were more likely to identify children with chronic illnesses, such as diabetes ($r = -0.52$, $p = 0.00$) and asthma ($r = -0.43$, $p = 0.00$).

- Districts with lower ratios reported more psychosocial services available and given to students (r = -0.38, p = 0.00).
- In districts with good student-to-nurse ratios, 70 percent of the building staff were trained as first responders, compared to 30 percent in districts with poor student-to-nurse ratios.
- Districts with lower ratios had a higher number of children receiving care for vision screening (r = -0.37, p = 0.007).

Research on School Psychologists

Psychologists perform a variety of services in the school depending on what model they are under, traditional or problem-solving. One study indicated that psychologists with a traditional role spend 51 percent of their time on assessments (Nelson & Gardner, 1998). Other services include counseling, behavioral intervention, systemic intervention, affective education, crisis intervention, program evaluation, consultation, and parent training. Little empirical research has been found reporting the academic and/or achievement benefits for student performance.

Research on School Guidance and Counseling

Johnson and Johnson (2003) recognized the need for counselors to answer the accountability question, "How are students different as a result of the guidance program?" (p. 181). To effectively answer this question, the *American Association of School Counselors* has created a comprehensive list of appropriate and inappropriate activities in which the school counselor should or should not be engaged. The URL (see Resources) succinctly identified the types of services that effective school counseling provided their schools. Additionally, the site lists Sabella's well-thought-out interview questions to use when hiring a counselor. Many of the forty-two questions could easily be tied to program evaluation.

Lapan, Gysbers, and Petroski (2003) found that a comprehensive guidance and counseling program supported positive student relationships with teachers. Students reported feeling safe and experiencing success. Seventh graders reported a relationship between the types of relationships they had with their teachers and counselors and their attitudes toward school. Positive teacher relationships resulted in positive experiences in school. These students also reported feeling safer, earning higher grades, and believing in the importance of an education. Conversely, they reported that in the positive teacher-relationship environments, there were fewer academic distractions because of peers acting out, misbehaving, or disrupting class. Schools that offered a comprehensive guidance program were also found to engage larger numbers of students in activities that fostered positive relationships (Wentzel, 1999).

Lapan, Gysbers, and Petroski (2003) reported that low-income schools with a comprehensive guidance program had students that also recognized the importance of education. Additionally, they recognized the relevance of the nurturing relationships they had with their teachers. However, these same students from high-poverty schools (including minority) reported dissatisfaction with the quality of life available at their schools. They reported that too much class time was wasted, interrupted, noisy, and set at uncomfortable temperatures. They did not feel safe at school, did less homework, and reported earning lower grades. The study concluded that a comprehensive guidance program benefited seventh graders, regardless of their income levels.

Nelson and Gardner (1998) found that high schools with comprehensive guidance and counseling programs reported students took more advanced math and science courses and scored higher on the ACT College Entrance Examination.

Counselors who worked in schools rated as excellent provided more services than those in average or below-average schools. A review of the literature on school guidance counselors by Borders and Drury (1992) identified three main roles that affect student outcomes: counseling, classroom guidance, and consultation. Several studies found that students who received counseling improved their academic achievement.

Lee (1993) found classroom guidance had a positive effect on academic achievement. Carns and Carns (1991) reported that a study skills guidance activity resulted in an increase of three years and one month improvement in academic achievement. There are several positive effects of group counseling: (1) increase in academic persistence and achievement, (2) increase in school attendance, (3) better classroom behavior, (4) higher self-esteem, and (5) increased number of positive attitudes toward school. Borders and Drury (1992) reported that counseling was effective with special population groups, such as: gifted students, students from divorces families, learning-disabled students, and disruptive students. Peer facilitation is effective in improving classroom behaviors and school attitudes of elementary school children. Teachers who participated in the consultation process tended to create more **positive learning environments**, complimented students more, had more positive interactions with students, and reported higher job satisfaction.

The research documents the relationship between student achievement and parent involvement. Parent education programs have shown positive effects on achievement and attitudes toward self and others, and additional positive influences were reported on preschool students, elementary students, African American elementary students, rural students, low-socioeconomic students, low-achieving students, suburban students, upper-middle class students, learning-disabled students, and children of divorced parents.

Classroom Guidance

Some research has demonstrated the positive effects of classroom guidance on student outcomes (Borders & Drury, 1992). Both teachers and students reported positive changes in attitudes and classroom behavior for targeted students (poor initial attitudes) and top students. No specific improvements were made in achievement, but improvement in classroom behavior and attitudes were reported. After completing a guidance session on exam preparation, sixth-grade students scored higher on final exams than those without the course. Lee (1993) examined the Success for School program and found significant increases in mathematics test scores, but no significant difference in reading achievement or school attitudes.

RESEARCH ON SCHOOL SOCIAL WORKERS

The National Association of School Social Workers (2002), Standard 11, states:

School social workers shall maintain accurate data that are relevant to planning, management, and evaluation of school social work services.

Timely and accurate records document school social work services, demonstrate outcomes, and promote accountability to the local education
agency and community. Analyses of activity reports, program statistics,
and outcome measures can support the effective use of school social work
services to better meet the needs of students and families. (p. 15)

Dibble (1999) identified the need for accountability and results. He
stated, "Outcome evaluation is about what tangible, positive changes
have occurred that are to a substantial degree due to the provision of
your school social work services" (p. 7). In addition, he recommended
alignment of school social worker outcomes to the school/district
goal(s) through the development of an evaluation plan. To develop an
effective plan, Dibble suggested the following questions as important
to answer:

1. *Who is your audience? What stakeholders are you trying to influence? To whom will you present the findings of your outcome
   evaluation? What does your audience value? What established
   priorities or goals does your audience have?* Your audience is
   the people to whom you are accountable. . . . The demonstrated
   positive outcomes of your school social work services need to
   be consistent with what your audience thinks is important for
   your school district to accomplish. Almost all school districts
   have written goals that they use as benchmarks to determine if
   they are making progress in identified priority areas, (e.g., academic achievement, graduation rates, attendance rates, parent
   involvement.).

2. *Which one or more of your audience's established priorities or
   goals do your school social work services* **tangibly and significantly** *impact?* Outcome evaluation is not about counting how
   many home visits were made, support groups were facilitated,
   or developmental histories were completed, although this kind
   of data is relatively easy to collect and is useful in documenting
   what you do. Outcome evaluation is about what tangible, positive changes have occurred that are to a substantial degree due
   to the provision of your school social work services. Another
   way to look at this is to ask yourself, if my school social work
   services were not provided, would significantly less progress be

made on any of the school district's priorities or goals? . . . The greater the impact of your school social work services on any given goal, the more power and influence your results will have on your audience.

3. *What data does your school system presently collect that can help document progress on your audience's priorities and goals? What data is available to you? What data is easily obtainable?*

4. *Which of the identified data are appropriate indicators of the success or progress of one or more of your school social work services?* Of the data you have listed in step #3, which are **significantly and tangibly** impacted by your services? The more reasonable it is for your audience to believe that your services impact the data you are presenting to them, the more likely it is they will conclude the positive changes in the data are at least in part attributable to your services.

5. *Which of the identified data indicators from step #4 that a) address one or more of your audience's priorities, and b) are significantly and tangibly impacted by one or more of your services, will you use and analyze?* Briefly describe the rationale you will use to link each type of data to your school social work services. (pp. 7–8)

It would seem that the need to provide evidence of effectiveness has been realized. It is a positive sign when internal agents recognize the need for their profession to respond to the need for empirical evidence of impact.

Consultative Process

A common thread throughout all of the support services research was the need for a strong consultative process. Dame (1994) reported a positive impact on student achievement as a result of the collaborative-consultative service delivery model. This model incorporates the collaboration across disciplines and professions. This **non-territorial approach** seeks to provide the highest quality of prevention and/or intervention possible for the student and his/her family. Consultation process research also found that guidance counselor consultation with teachers, parents, or both improved academic achievement, attention, classroom behaviors, motivation, and student self-concept. Behavior consultation is especially effective in changing inappropriate behaviors. Teachers trained in facilitative skills have students with better achievement, attendance, and self-concepts (Borders & Drury, 1992).

The reauthorization of Individuals with Disabilities Education Improvement Act (IDEIA) in 2004 (originally *Public Law* 94-0142) requires states to allow districts to adopt alternative models for classification of learning disabilities. Many states are implementing the response to intervention model, also known as the problem-solving model (Wedl, 2005). The model is supported through a comprehensive collaborative approach, using data and science-based research strategies and programs. Student support personnel will have a key role in the effective implementation in the identification of the problem, etiology of the problem, suggested interventions, and objectively evaluating the progress.

QUESTIONS FOR REFLECTION AND DISCUSSION

1. What evaluation system do we have in place for all student support personnel?
2. What job descriptions are in place for the student support personnel?
3. How is the effectiveness of their service delivery model evaluated on an annual basis?
4. How well are the student support services coordinated both at the building and district levels? Is there duplication of services?
5. How well do the student support personnel collaborate with classroom teachers and administrators?
6. How effective are the student support personnel in intervening with families?
7. How effective are student support personnel in public relations and the marketing of the school and the district?
8. Who is evaluating the response to intervention model for local impact?

DATA SETS

Data sets for student support services can be reported monthly, quarterly, and/or annually, depending on the district's needs. All departments should be required to report SMART goals for continuous improvement, reports on the progress of those goals, and data supporting the accomplishment of those goals.

Related to All

1. What types of evaluation surveys are completed by teachers, students, and others on the services provided by the support staff (i.e., customer service, effectiveness of services, availability, professionalism, collaboration)?
2. How many active student cases does each support staff carry?
3. How many referrals are waiting to receive active case status?
4. How many classroom teacher consultations/contacts were made?
5. How many staffings were they actively engaged in?
6. How many classroom observations were conducted?
7. How many interdistrict or community-based services were provided?

School Nurse

1. How many new students were placed on medication?
2. How many different types of medications are administered at school?
3. How many health awareness or health preparedness sessions were held with students? How many with families?
4. Report the data on student vision and hearing testing results. As a result of your screenings, how many students were referred for vision and hearing testing? How many students received treatment (glasses, hearing aids, referral for additional services)?
5. What health needs/issues are being monitored in each building?

6. How many health needs/issues are being monitored in each building?
7. How many absences are health related? Is there a pattern of the types, times, days of the weeks?
8. How many tardies are health-related? Is there a pattern of the types, times, days of the weeks?
9. How many students with allergies are you monitoring? What is the breakdown of the types of allergies (i.e., bee stings, food allergies, etc.)?

School Social Worker

1. How many home visits are conducted?
2. How many parenting workshops are conducted? What did the workshop evaluations report? What impact or result(s) are expected?
3. How many students received interventions? What was the result of the intervention(s) (i.e., improved attendance, homework turned in on time, controlled "reactions," etc.)?
4. How many collaborative intervention sessions were held? What were the outcome(s) of these sessions?

School Psychologist

1. How many classroom observations were conducted? What were the results of those visits?
2. How many student behavior reports were filed?
3. How many interventions were provided to students, teachers, families? What were the outcomes?

Speech Therapist

1. How many classroom interventions occurred?
2. How many sessions of whole-class and small-group instructions take place within the regular classroom?
3. How many students were staffed into speech therapy?
4. How many students were staffed out of speech therapy?

SUMMARY OF STUDENT SUPPORT SERVICES

There is no denying the importance of the social, emotional, psychological, and physical needs of our children. It is up to the adults in their world to ensure that necessary balance exists for each one of them. What is there to gain if the United States commands first place in the global science, math, and technology race if our children are overweight, physically ill, emotionally maladjusted (unhappy, depressed, suicidal, selfish, mean-spirited), and not centered maturing individuals?

Attention must not be blindly focused on test scores but also on healthy modeling with expectations of the development of well-rounded children. It is also imperative that individual programs within schools, such as counseling, school psychologists, speech therapists, social workers, and nurses, work together toward the common good of all children. Territorialism is counterproductive and a negative model for children to witness.

RESOURCES FOR CONTINUED EXPLORATION OF STUDENT SUPPORT SERVICES

The National Association of School Social Workers: National Standards of School Social Worker Services. http://www.socialworkers.org/practice/standards/NASW_SSWS.pdf

Dibble, N. (1999). *Outcome evaluation of school social work services.* Retrieved June 18, 2007, from http://dpi.state.wi.us/sspw/pdf/outcmeval999.pdf

The National Association of School Nurses. http://www.nasn.org/

The American Association of Speech and Hearing Therapists. http://www.asha.org/default.htm

The American Association of School Counselors. http://www.schoolcounselor.org/

(10)

SCHOOL SAFETY—NOT AN OPTIONAL ACTIVITY

Don't learn safety rules simply by accident.

ThinkExist.com

The safety of the people shall be the highest law.

Cicero

ESSENTIAL QUESTION

How do you ensure a safe, orderly, caring, and healthy school environment?

DEFINITIONS

School violence—The Center for the Prevention of School Violence, a resource center and think tank, describes school violence as any *behavior that violates a school's educational mission or climate of respect or jeopardizes the intent of the school to be free of aggression against persons or property, drugs, weapons, disruptions, and disor-*

der (North Carolina Department of Juvenile Justice and Delinquency Prevention, 2002, p. 1).

Data from the *National Crime Victimization Survey* (2004, p. 14) indicated that students between the ages of twelve to eighteen were victims of 1.4 million nonfatal crimes while in school and 1.3 million crimes while away from school. In 2004, there were 583,000 twelve- to eighteen-year-old victims of violent crimes, and 863,000 thefts were experienced at school (p. ix). In 2005, 25 percent of students in grades nine through twelve reported that drugs were made available on school property, while 8 percent were threatened or injured with a weapon on school property.

What level of progress has been made in the effort to reduce violence and increase safety? The *Indicators of School Crime and Safety* (2006) asserted that school safety has improved. Data such as the victimization rate (which decreased for students twelve to eighteen year olds from 73 victimizations per 1,000 in 2003 to 55 per 1,000 in 2004 also showed improvment). Although progress has been made in some areas, the report also noted that from July 1, 2004, to July 30, 2005, there were 48 school-associated violent deaths in elementary and secondary schools in America (p. ix). The existence of discipline problems in a school may contribute to an environment that facilitates school violence and crime (Miller, 2003). Other areas of concern are physical fighting, use of drugs and alcohol, and carrying weapons, all of which impact the safety and learning environment in America's schools.

Bullying—aggressive behavior that is intentional and involves an imbalance of power or strength, unprovoked and repeated over time (Olweus, 2004). It includes common types of harassment such as name-calling, making fun of others, spreading nasty rumors, and shoving and kicking. It crosses all ethnic and socioeconomic groups.

Twenty-eight percent of students twelve to eighteen years of age reported being bullied at school. Nineteen percent said they had been made fun of by a bully, 15 percent had been the subject of rumors, and 9 percent had been spit on, pushed, and/or tripped. Seventy-nine percent had been bullied within the walls of the school and 28 percent had been bullied outside of school (Dinkes et al., 2006). Bullying is most likely to occur in schools where teachers and students are indifferent to or accept bullying behavior (Learning First Alliance, 2001), especially during breaks when adult supervision is lacking and when rules against bullying are inconsistently enforced (Olweus, 2004). While approaches that simply crack down on individual bullies are seldom effective, if there is a school-wide commitment to end bullying, it can be reduced by up to 50 percent.

Cyber-bullying—a growing, national, school safety issue. Cyber-bullying is online social cruelty or electronic bullying and can involve sending mean, vulgar, or threatening messages or images; posting sensitive or private information about another person on the Internet; and/or sending emails using another student's name (Willard, 2005).

Students are using the Internet as an instrument of intimidation, embarrassment, threats, ridicule, and hatred. Wolak, Mitchell, and Finkelhor (2006) found in their report for the National Center for Missing and Exploited Children that twice as many children and youth indicated that they had been victims and perpetrators of online harassment in 2005 compared with 1999/2000.

Gang—a group of individuals, juveniles, and/or adults who associate on a continuous basis, form an allegiance with a common purpose, and are involved in delinquent or criminal behaviors/activity (please note that there is a lack of agreement among professionals regarding this definition).

Twenty-four percent of students reported that there were gangs at their school. The reported increase of the presence of gangs in urban (36 percent), suburban (21 percent), and rural (16 percent) school campuses is cause for alarm (Dinkes, et al., 2006). Howell and Lynch (2000) stated, "The presence of gangs is correlated with criminal activity and the use of self-protective measures that indicate an atmosphere of perceived danger in the school environment" (p. 7). Welsh, Gren, and Jenkins (1999) found that gangs and criminal victimization in schools are products of disorder in schools. This is another reason why culture and climate are significant, even when dealing with gang-related issues.

School Climate—a feeling generated by the atmosphere and personality within the building. It is multidimensional, including such factors as physical appearance and structure of the building, student interpersonal relationships, student-teacher relationships, the sharing of resources, achievement motivation, order and discipline, and parent involvement (Marshall, n.d.).

School Culture—the behind-the-scenes context that reflects the values, beliefs, norms, traditions, and rituals that build up over time as people in a school work together. It influences not only the actions of the school population, but also its motivations and spirit (Peterson, 2002).

RESEARCH: WHAT WE KNOW ABOUT WHAT WORKS?

More significant than academic achievement is the responsibility that leadership has to provide a safe and supportive learning environment. In light of the last two decades of highly publicized school shootings, schools have been forced to look for quick fixes. Subsequently, millions of dollars have been spent on hardware. Such reactive measures include the use of cameras/video monitoring, ID badges with automatic readers, wand and walk-through metal detectors, motion detectors, and duress alarms. Additionally, zero-tolerance policies, automatic suspensions, mandatory school uniforms, random locker checks, locked schoolhouse doors, non-police hall monitors, and extra police patrols/school safety officer (Hyman & Perone, 1998; Jones, 2006; Lockwood, 1997; http://www.secretservice.gov/ntac_ssi.shtml) have also been implemented by schools and districts. School safety has quickly become a multibillion dollar business.

> What's in? Handheld communications and data storage gadgetry. Community antiviolence summits. Biometric recognition equipment. Increased training and certification for school resource officers. "Shelter in place." Arts-based prevention intervention. Conflict-resolution skills development. School crisis planning. "Online social cruelty." Truancy focus. Anti-bullying laws. Risk management analysis. (Colgan, 2005, p. 10)

In many of the sites where fatal shootings have occurred, all or a combination of these tools/interventions were in place. Yet school violence continues to be a major social issue. Are schools doing everything they can to keep their students and staff safe?

No problem as serious as school violence has a simple solution. School violence is not only a school problem, to be solved by board policies, hardware, training manuals, practice drills, but it is a community problem. Such issues as poverty, family stress, poor job forecasts for young people, violence in the media, uncontrolled access to guns and drugs (Sheley & Wright, 1998), bullying, a lack of role models effectively using conflict-resolution skills, and a lack of personal relationships (Olweus, 2004; Smith, Pepler, & Rigby, 2004; stopbullyingnow.hrsa.gov, 2007) all impact students' sense of well-being and security.

Much has been learned about what effective school safety entails. One such study (Fein et al., 2002) was a collaboration between the U.S. Department of Education and the U.S. Secret Service. The resulting study examined the incidences of school violence from 1974 to 2000 (the report can be downloaded from http://www.secretservice.gov/ntac_ssi.shtml). The top-two risk factors were a history of victimization and isolation. There is no accurate profile for the identification of perpetrators, but often overlooked are students that have been bullied. The U.S. Department of Education, Office of OSERS/OSEP, states the following warning on their Web site:

> Early warning signs can help frame concern for a child. However, it is important to avoid inappropriately labeling or stigmatizing individual students because they appear to fit a specific profile or set of early warning indicators. It's okay to be worried about a child, but it's not okay to overreact and jump to conclusions. (Dwyer, Osher, & Warger, 1998, p. 6)

The report cautions against using any list of descriptors to "identify or profile" a potentially dangerous student; to do so is counterproductive and illegal.

The Effective Schools research (2002) reported that a safe, orderly, caring environment and parent involvement are essential for students to achieve. Fein et al. (2002) found in the Secret Service study on threat assessment that, "creating climates of school safety was a foundation for reducing school violence" (p. 15). A positive school culture respects the rights and emotions of every individual within the building, radiates high expectations for student achievement, is collaborative, flexible, and honors the uniqueness of every child. A positive school climate possesses administrators with an open-door policy; children and adults who want to be at school, a feeling of optimism permeates the building; clearly identified rules and practices; facilities that are in good physical condition, clean, and environmentally healthy; small class size support; behavioral issues that are handled quickly and fairly; and all adults alert to the needs of all children (Gunzelmann, 2004). Fein et al. (2002) also added the need for students to "break the code of silence" (p. 17). The report found that students were more willing to discuss their own pain or the pain of a classmate if the environment is positioned with caring adults who listen.

Research indicates that it is the establishment of "human relationships" that work best to reduce the chances of extreme violence (Olweus, 2004; Smith, Pepler, & Rigby, 2004; stopbullyingnow.hrsa.gov, 2007). School climates that are environments of collaboration and sharing encourage intellectual risk-taking, allow students to receive the assistance needed to become successful, contributing members of the school and community, and when relationships are the focus of all that is accomplished, these schools reduce discipline and de-escalate violence. When the focus is on positive interpersonal relationships and the development of optimal learning opportunities for *all* students, this results in increased achievement levels and reduced maladaptive behavior (Harris & Lowery, 2002; McEvoy & Welker, 2000; Peterson & Skiba, 2001). Research-based strategies must be incorporated into the school and district improvement plans, and focus on meeting the needs of *all* students.

One approach that has been shown to effectively change the school culture is parental and community involvement in the school. By involving teachers and parents in the supervision of nonacademic time, raising stakeholder awareness about bullying, forming clear rules and strong social norms against bullying, and providing support and protection for all students, the culture informs students that they are important. Changing the culture involves all stakeholders (teachers, principals, students, and support staff, such as janitors, cafeteria workers, and crossing guards). The more that data on bullying and student perceptions of their safety is shared, the greater the communities' involvement in changing the situation. By all stakeholders celebrating differences, and honoring diversity, school violence and be prevented. Students pledge not to bully other students, to help students who are bullied, and to make a point to include students who are often left out (Olweus, Limber, & Mihalic, 1999).

Threat Assessment

The Secret Service (Fein et al., 2002) definition of threat assessment is a process of identifying, assessing, and managing the threat that certain persons may pose to Secret Service protectees. You must intervene before an actual attack occurs. This usually involves three steps: (1) identifying the individual(s) who pose a threat, (2) using information from multiple sources to determine whether the individual is to a threat or not, and (3) when a person is determined to be a threat, managing the threat the individual poses.

NATIONAL CENTER FOR SCHOOL SAFETY CHECKLIST

These characteristics should serve to alert school administrators, teachers, and support staff to address needs of troubled students through meetings with parents, school counselors, guidance and mentoring staff, as well as referrals to appropriate community health/social services and law-enforcement personnel. Further, such behavior should also provide an early warning signal that safe school plans and crisis prevention/intervention procedures must be in place to protect the health and safety of all school students and staff members so that schools remain safe havens for learning.

_____ Has a history of tantrums and uncontrollable angry outbursts.

_____ Characteristically resorts to name calling, cursing, or abusive language.

_____ Habitually makes violent threats when angry.

_____ Has previously brought a weapon to school.

_____ Has a background of serious disciplinary problems at school and in the community.

_____ Has a background of drug, alcohol, or other substance abuse or dependency.

_____ Is on the fringe of his/her peer group with few or no close friends.

_____ Is preoccupied with weapons, explosives, or other incendiary devices.

_____ Has previously been truant, suspended, or expelled from school.

_____ Displays cruelty to animals.

_____ Has little or no supervision and support from parents or a caring adult.

_____ Has witnessed or been a victim of abuse or neglect in the home.

_____ Has been bullied and/or bullies or intimidates peers or younger children.

_____ Tends to blame others for difficulties and problems s/he causes her/himself.

_____ Consistently prefers TV shows, movies, or music expressing violent themes and acts.

_____ Prefers reading materials dealing with violent themes, rituals, and abuse.

_____ Reflects anger, frustration, and the dark side of life in school essays or writing projects.

_____ Is involved with a gang or an antisocial group on the fringe of peer acceptance.

_____ Is often depressed and/or has significant mood swings.

_____ Has threatened or attempted suicide (National Center for School Safety Checklist, 1998, p. 7).

QUESTIONS FOR DISCUSSION AND REFLECTION

1. What school safety discipline data are collected and analyzed, and how is it used for proactive decision-making and problem-solving?
2. Does the school/district utilize the threat assessment in schools or a guide to ascertain threats to school safety?
3. Are school climate inventories administered, analyzed, interpreted, and utilized?
4. Does a procedure exist for students and others to report teacher bullying (McEvoy, 2005; Tremlow, Fonagy, Sacco, & Brethour, 2006)?
5. How often is the school safety plan updated and faculty/staff kept current?
6. Are students experiencing social and emotional problems offered individual and group counseling and are parents included?

7. How have personnel been trained to identify and work with these students?
8. What board policies exist related to school safety? How often are they updated?
9. How are schools/districts utilizing the expertise of the community to continuously improve on school safety measures?
10. How are community agencies (such as the police department, fire department, health department, mental health departments, hospitals, and emergency service personnel) involved in the design and implementation of the school safety plan?
11. What data do we have and use that informs us that our expenditures for metal detectors, cameras, and school-resource officers improve school safety?

DATA SETS THAT COULD BE REPORTED

Colgan (2005) reported that the lack of data on school safety is part of the problem. Data must be collected and *analyzed* for patterns and trends. The data must be examined at the district, building, and the individual student level.

Administrators must analyze the data in terms of trends. Analysis must include more than just completing and filing the annual school safety report. Data should be reported monthly, quarterly, each semester, or annually. Keep in mind the farther out these data are reported

Table 10.1.

	SES	Gender		W	AA	His.	AmI	Asian	O	SpEd
		M	F							
Attendance										
In-school suspension										
Out of school suspensions										
Assaults on staff										
Assaults on students										
Firearms & weapons										
Bomb threats										
Arrests										
Expulsions										

from the offense, the more difficult change/improvement is to make. Look for patterns and/or trends by examining multiple variables, such as race, grade level, age, program status (gifted, Title I, special education, regular division), and SES.

1. Who are the repeat offenders? (3–5 percent) _____

2. Who refers students? _____

3. What are you doing about it? _____

4. Location and time of the incidences: _____

5. Frequency, intensity, and duration of episodes of aggression: ____
   _____

6. How often are students polled for incidences of bullying? _____
   _____

7. What does the district Board of Education policy say about bully-ing or cyber-bullying? _____

8. By grade level, how many students were bullied each quarter?
   _____

9. How many incidences of cyber-bullying occur each quarter?
   _____

10. How often are the counselors evaluated by students, teachers, and parents for impact, availability, knowledge, and effective-ness? _____

11. How many parent training sessions on bullying, cyber-bullying, and conflict resolution were taken? _____

12. How many parent volunteers serve within each building? _____
    _____

13. How many parent volunteers serve outside of the regular school day? _____

14. How many students were referred for drug treatment? _____
    _____

15. How many students received their first discipline referral for misconduct (by gender, race, teacher, time of incident—look for the patterns)? _____

16. How many students received discipline referrals for misconduct that has been ongoing and repeated? _____
    What types of interventions have been provided for these stu-dents? _____

17. Are adults at each building expected to follow the same rules that the students are expected to follow? What rewards and consequences exist for faculty?

SUMMARY

Communities must address the larger social contextual issues, such as poverty, bullying, media, and unemployment, while the schools *must* address the needs of the whole child. If we are to improve school safety, then we must do more than react. We must assume responsibility for the development of the whole child through focusing on the psychological, emotional, moral, physical, and intellectual developments of our students. More importantly, as many adults as possible must model effective problem-solving strategies, conflict-resolution techniques, and healthy communication skills.

RESOURCES FOR CONTINUED EXPLORATION

Office of Safe and Drug Free Schools. Online Workshops: Drug & Violence Prevention Web Courses for Schools. http://www.ed.gov/admins/lead/safety /training/index.html

National Center for School Safety Checklist of Characteristics of Youth Who Have Caused School Associated Violent Deaths. Retrieved September 9, 2006, from http://www.schoolsafety.us/Checklist-of-Characteristics-of-Youth-Who-Have-Caused-School-Associated-Violent-Deaths-p-7.html

NetSmart—Parents' and guardians' premier, online resource for answering questions about Internet safety, computers, and the Web (http://www .netsmartz411.org/CAisd/pdmweb.exe).

Quest. http://www.incredibleinternet.com/index.php/do/online_safety

Cyberbullying: A growing problem. Great information about what to do and where to report cyberbullying (http://www.cybertipline.com or by calling 1–800–843–5678).

Richardson, J. (2001, April/May). School culture survey. *Tools For Schools*, *3*. This survey can be used with school staffs to assess underlying norms and values. The survey provides an excellent tool for assessing the culture.

Resource on bullying—http://stopbullyingnow.hrsa.gov/adult/indexAdult.asp?Area=acknowledegments

Stop Bullying Now—Great materials to use with students, including online webisodes (http://stopbullyingnow.hrsa.gov/index.asp?Area=webisodes&we bisodes).

Center for Effective Collaboration and Practice—http://cecp.air.org/guide/web-sites.asp

Center for Juvenile Justice: Law Enforcement Training and Technical Assistance. Developing an anti-bullying program (http://www.theiacp.org/Train-ing/bullyingbrief.pdf).

11

EXTENDED LEARNING PROGRAMS: BEFORE SCHOOL, AFTER SCHOOL, INTERSESSION, SATURDAY AND SUMMER SCHOOL—CAN MORE BE BETTER?

Yesterday is not ours to recover, but tomorrow is ours to win or lose.

Lyndon B. Johnson

ESSENTIAL QUESTION

What evidence do we have that extended learning is making a difference in short- and long-term student achievement?

DEFINITIONS

Out-of-school time/program **(OST/OSP)**—programs and learning opportunities that take place outside of the regular school day (figure 11.1).

Extended learning—this term encompasses all of the programs and learning opportunities held after school or during evening school, before school, in Saturday school, and summer school.

Summer school—programs and opportunities held during the summer months to enhance students' academic, social, and personal growth.

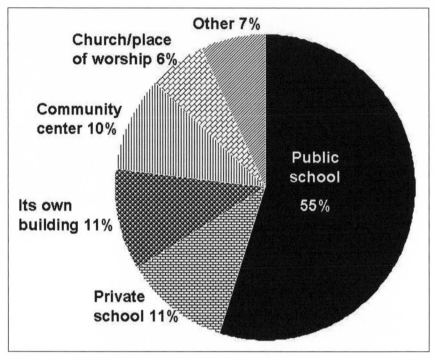

Chart 11.1. Percentage of Kindergarten through Eighth-Grade Children Attending Before-and/or After-School Center- or School-Based Programs.

Intersession—periods in the calendar when year-round schools are not in session and where programs and opportunities may be offered to enhance academic, social, and personal growth of students.

RESEARCH

In 2005, the National Center for Educational Statistics (NCES) reported that 40 percent of students in kindergarten through eighth grade were in at least one weekly nonparental after-school care arrangement. The U.S. Census Bureau (2006) reported that one third of all school-age children in the United States, for some part of the week, go home to an empty house or apartment. The total number may be between five and seven million children between five and thirteen years old. Some researchers estimate the number closer to sixteen million children. The

Census Bureau found that 15 percent were home alone before school, 76 percent after school, and 9 percent at night.

One half of all children in the country age twelve to fourteen are home alone an average of seven hours a week. The very poor in America are less likely to leave their children alone at home, or allow them to go home alone, than families who earn twice the poverty income. This is probably because the very poor live in less-safe neighborhoods and have fewer friends or family who can step in, in case of emergency. In spite of the hours spent on the job, working mothers spend an average of five-and-a-half hours a day with their children.

Alston (2006) describes these latch-key children (U.S. Census Bureau, 2006):

- Fifty-one percent are doing poorly in school. Most teachers believe that being alone at home is the number one cause of school failure.
- Afternoon hours are the peak time for juvenile crime. In the last eleven years, juvenile crime has increased 48 percent.
- The Carnegie Council on Adolescent Development found that eighth graders who are alone eleven hours a week are twice as likely to abuse drugs as adolescents who are busy after school. The Council also found that teens who have sexual intercourse do it in the afternoon in the home of boys whose parents work.
- Unsupervised children are more likely to become depressed, smoke cigarettes and marijuana, and drink alcohol.
- Latch-key children are more likely to be the victims of crimes. When home alone, latch-key children generally watch television, eat snacks, play with pets, and fight with siblings.

Districts and communities offer a variety of extended learning programs and opportunities for students to supplement their education. Before school, after school, evening school, Saturday, and/or summer school programs provide students with a wide range of academic and personal growth opportunities. The only legal mandate for extended learning opportunities before the No Child Left Behind (NCLB) Act (2001) was Public Law 94-142 for special-education students, which gave rise to summer school programs, extending the learning for students with disabilities who were not progressing satisfactorily. Wrightslaw: Special Education Law-IDEA 2004 regulations Section .300.309 stipulated that extended school year services must be provided if the IEP team determines that the services are necessary under the provision of FAPE (Free Appropriate Public Education).

With the onset of the NCLB Act of 2001, schools that were not making adequate yearly progress after three years were required to provide supplemental educational services outside of the school day. This has also given rise to more rigorous program-evaluation data because the provider of the service must demonstrate that students are making satisfactory growth in academic achievement. The Elementary and Secondary Education Act (ESEA) of 1965 also provided an impetus for summer school and after-school programs through Title I dollars. Funds were provided to low-income schools to assist districts and schools in providing supplemental services to low-income students.

Cooper, Charlton, Valentine, and Muhlenbruck (2000) conducted a meta-analysis (which "combines the result of several studies that address a set of related research questions" [WikiPedia, para. 1]) of summer school programs and drew the following research conclusions:

- Summer-school programs focused on lessening or removing learning deficiencies have a positive impact on the knowledge and skills of participants (students can be expected to score about one-fifth of a standard deviation higher than the control group on outcome measures) (Cooper et al., 2000, p. 8).
- Summer-school programs focused on acceleration of learning or on other goals have a positive impact on participants, roughly equal to programs focusing on remedial goals.
- Summer-school programs have more positive effects on the achievement of middle-class students than on students from disadvantage backgrounds.
- Remedial summer programs have larger positive effects when the program is run for a small number of school/classes or in a small community, although the largest programs showed positive average effects.
- Summer programs that provide small-group or individual instruction produced the largest impact on student outcomes.

Additional findings from this study included five other conclusions, but the authors stated that these were presented with less confidence. The other findings included: some form of parental involvement produced larger effects; a larger effect on mathematics achievement than on reading; the achievement in summer school may diminish over time; and remedial summer-school program had positive effects for all grade levels, but the effects were more pronounced for students in the elementary grades and secondary schools than in middle schools. The authors also noted that the meta-analysis showed clear and reliable benefits of summer school for students with disabilities, and they noted that remedial programs requiring attendance are more effective than voluntary programs (2000).

A recent (Lauer et al., 2007) meta-analysis on out-of-school programs for at-risk students concluded that these programs have positive effects on at-risk students' achievement in reading and mathematic. The results also indicated that program duration and student grouping influenced program effectiveness. One of the strongest findings in this meta-analysis was the positive effect of one-on-one tutoring for at-risk students on reading achievement. This study also indicated that K-12 students benefited from out-of-school programs for improved reading. There were also indicators that mathematics achievement primarily occurred at the secondary grades. The authors concluded that OSP programs do not need to focus solely on academic activities in order to have positive effects on student achievement. Their analysis indicated that programs where activities were both academic and social realized positive influences on student achievement. The authors recommended that administrators of these programs should monitor the implementation and ongoing student learning to determine the appropriate investment of time for specific strategies and activities (Lauer et al., 2006).

Durlak and Weissberg (2007) conducted a meta-analysis on after-school programs that focused on enhancing personal and social skills. The programs that they evaluated targeted problem-solving, conflict resolution, self-control, leadership, responsible decision-making, and enhancement of self-efficacy and self esteem. The most significant findings from this study were:

- Students who participated in after-school programs improved significantly in three areas: feeling and attitudes, indicators of behavioral adjustment, *and* school performance. Resulting behaviors impacted were self-confidence, self-esteem, school bonding, positive social behaviors, grades, and performance on achievement tests. Problem behaviors were reduced along with drug use.

• Effective after-school programs were identified. "Programs that used evidence-based skill training approaches were consistently successful in producing multiple benefits for youth, while those that did not use such procedures were not successful in any outcome area" (p. 7).

Results of evaluation summaries on thirteen out-of-school programs funded by the Mott Foundation in 2003 indicated that eleven of the thirteen programs realized academic achievement outcomes for young people (p. 17). In addition, eight of the thirteen programs reported improved school attendance outcomes for youth (p. 17). The Quantum Opportunities Program students became teen parents less often, and they had a third less children. They were also less likely to be arrested and were involved in fewer total crimes (p. 19).

The largest, federal, after-school programs study, *When Schools Stay Open Late: The National Evaluation of the 21st Century Community Learning Centers Programs*, included sixty-two middle school centers in thirty-four school districts and thirty-four elementary school centers in fourteen school districts. Key findings at the elementary level included limited academic impact with the exception of social studies grades and no impact on elementary students completing their homework to their teacher's satisfaction. In addition, there were no improvements in safety and behavior; however, there was increased parental involvement at the middle school, and parents of elementary students were more likely to help with homework or ask about classroom activities.

The program evaluation also reported that there appeared to be no impact on planning or goal setting for the students or on their ability to work as team members. And middle school students were less likely to view themselves as "good" or "excellent" at working out conflicts with others.

Out-of-school opportunities help children and adolescents fill their time with productive activities. Many times when children and adolescents are not provided structure with their unsupervised time, they do not use their time wisely.

QUESTIONS FOR REFLECTION AND DISCUSSION

1. How are students identified for summer-school and after-school programs and opportunities? Are the referrals only related to failing grades and performance on standardized achievement tests?
2. What evidence can be provided that parental involvement is a significant part of the after-school and the summer-school experience?
3. What are the desired outcomes for student participation in the programs and opportunities?
4. What data do we have that shows summer-school attendance influences student achievement as well as personal and social growth?
5. What data do we have that shows an academic, social, and/or emotional impact on student achievement as a result of participating in an after-school program?
6. What processes are in place for the planning, implementation, and coordination of the program to the instruction and curriculum of the academic day?
7. What form of assessment data is reported on individual student learning and achievement? Are report cards given?
8. If the extended learning program is tutorial, what training or technical support exists for the teachers?
9. If the extended learning program is instructional, what curriculum assessments are used?
10. Are parents, students, teachers, and administrators evaluating the effectiveness of the program?
11. What statement about priorities and caring are made by the location and facility(ies) of your out-of-school program?
12. How involved are the administrators in the planning process of the after-school program?
13. How involved are the students in the planning process of the out-of-school programs?
14. What needs have been identified for the targeted student populations (personal and social skills, such as conflict resolution, impulse control, and decision-making/problem solving)? What is being done to meet the identified need(s)? How is it being measured? To whom is it being reported?

15. How is the administration of the after-school/summer-school/out-of-school program being evaluated?
16. What is being done to motivate students to attend and participate? Whose responsibility is it?
17. How effectively are the community resources being integrated, coordinated, and/or utilized?
18. How many latch-key children are in our community? What agencies are working with them? How can or are these services coordinated for the greatest impact?
19. How is teaching performance evaluated?

After School Programs—Questions That Support Continuous Improvement

1. How do we assess the effectiveness of our after-school program? If we don't offer any extended learning opportunities, why not? If we do, how do we know whether it is working?

Summer School Programs—Questions That Support Continuous Improvement

1. How do we assess the effectiveness of summer school?
2. Is the curriculum and instruction rigorous (yet motivating) or simply viewed as meeting required seat time/attendance requirements?

If we don't offer summer school, how can we justify the lack of "anything" over the summer—we know that kids lose a lot over the three summer months—is that just "OK?"

DATA SETS THAT COULD BE REPORTED

Data sets that could be reported by all populations involved (i.e., gender, grade, race, income, programs such as Title I, special education, gifted, etc.) include:

1. Data from the needs assessment(s)—identifying what the stake-

holders (students, parents, teachers, community, administrators) feel are the interests and/or needs?

2. Out-of-school/extended learning attendance.
3. Pre- and posttesting results—reported as gain scores.
4. Entrance-level grades and exit-level grades.
5. Pre- and post-self-concept/esteem assessments.
6. Behavior (classroom, discipline—in-school suspensions, out-of-school suspensions, detentions, etc.).
7. School adjustment indicators.
8. Evidence of outreach programs/contacts with the home(s).
9. Evidence of parental involvement in the program.
10. Analysis of the progress reports.

SUMMARY

In conclusion, there are many fiscal, social, academic, and intellectual reasons for a community and its schools to provide out-of-school programming and services. The problems that arise when unsupervised adolescents spill out into our communities through acts of vandalism, violence, teen pregnancy, drug abuse, theft, and unlawful behaviors. The need for a high-quality after-school and summer-school experience, especially for high-poverty students, is well-documented and fiscally responsible.

RESOURCES FOR CONTINUED EXPLORATION

°*Measuring youth program quality: A guide to assessment tools.* (2007, March). http://www.forumfyi.org/Files/Measuring_Youth_Program _Quality.pdf

Activities and curriculum planning for five- to eleven-year-olds in out-of-school time programs. http://www.nationalserviceresources.org/resources /online_pubs/out-of-school_time/index.php

° All of the above resources are very good and will assist districts/schools in providing excellent extended learning experiences. This asterisk ° indicates an excellent source for program evaluation materials, resources, and research.

The impact of after-school programs that promote personal and social skills. (2007). Collaborative for Academic, Social, and Emotional Learning. http://www.casel.org/downloads/ASP-Exec.pdf

California 21st century high school safety and enrichment for teens (ASSETs) program. WestEd. http://www.wested.org/cs/we/view/rs/821

The effectiveness of out-of-school-time strategies in assisting low-achieving students in reading and mathematics: A research synthesis. (2007). McREL. http://www.mcrel.org/topics/products/151/

Harvard family research project out-of-school time program evaluation. http://www.gse.harvard.edu/hfrp/projects/afterschool/evaldatabase.html

Documenting progress and demonstrating results: Evaluating local out-of-school time programs. http://www.gse.harvard.edu/hfrp/content/projects/afterschool/resources/issuebried.pdf

Planning activities for out-of-school programs. Corporation of National and Community Service. http://nationalserviceresources.org/epicenter/practices/index.php?ep_action=view&ep_id=408

(12)

LEADERSHIP: SCHOOL BOARDS, ADMINISTRATION, AND TEACHER LEADERS—CHANGING ROLES FOR A CHANGING WORLD

Leadership is getting someone to do what they don't want to do, to achieve what they want to achieve.

Tom Landry

When one teaches, two learn.

Robert Half

ESSENTIAL QUESTIONS

In what ways do we model the level of excellence that we expect from our students, staff, and administration?

Are district, school, and board leaders focused on student outcomes?

DEFINITIONS

Leadership: Although there are many definitions of leadership, there are two that seem to represent the intention of all the others. First, by George Terry, who called it "the activity of influencing people to strive willingly for group goals," and second, John Pejza, who said, "You lead people; you manage things."

Instructional Leadership: A term that has become very popular within the last twenty years. Many definitions have been written, but we appreciate Blasé and Blasé's (1999) descriptors: facilitating collaborative efforts with teachers, establishing and supporting coaching relationships between teachers, using research to drive decision-making, knowing and using adult learning principles with teachers and support staff, and encouraging and facilitating the study of teaching and learning.

Teacher Leader: A certified teacher who assumes a leadership role. Lord and Miller (2000) stated, "teacher leader is a generic term, meaning different things to different people. To promote and support change in teachers' classroom practice" (p. 1).

Professional Learning Community (PLC): The adoption of a philosophy of teaching and learning that recognizes the need for a collaborative, student-focused culture. DuFour (2004) noted that PLCs focus on the power of questions, not answers. He suggested:

The school staff finds itself asking,

- What school characteristics and practices have been most successful in helping all students achieve at high levels?
- How could we adopt those characteristics and practices in our own school?
- What commitments would we have to make to one another to create such a school?
- What indicators could we monitor to assess our progress?

When the staff has built shared knowledge and found common ground on these questions, the school has a solid foundation for moving forward with its improvement initiative. (p. 6)

DuFour (2002) further identified three driving questions that professional learning communities must ask themselves in order to function as PLCs:

a) What do we want every student to know?

   b) How will we know it has been learned?
   c) How will we respond when a student experiences difficulty in learn-
       ing (p. 7)?

   His research indicated that the answer to (c) separates a PLC from
a traditional school.

Professional development: needs to be defined as opportunities to
   learn, rather than as training. "Opportunities to learn" means engagement in shared decision-making, inquiry, dialogue, reflection,
   community service, peer coaching and mediation, and workshops. *To*
   lead is to facilitate such learning toward a shared purpose. (Lambert,
   1998b, p. 88)

The twenty-first century will require a different type of leadership
(Black, 2006). The federal government's growing involvement in local
educational programming, funding, and accountability mandate the
necessity for exemplary educational leadership. Economic pressures,
global competitiveness, and a technologically advancing society dictates
that school boards, superintendents, building principals, and teacher
leaders demonstrate a stronger knowledge and skill basis in curriculum,
instruction, assessment, and accountability. These individuals must
know how to ask the critical questions regarding standards, assessment,
and student achievement. Suffice it to say that the status quo and just
meeting minimum expectations regardless of your current test scores
is no longer acceptable. Research clearly identifies the components of
effective leadership. Hiring decisions must be based on the research.
Leithwood, Seashore, Anderson, and Wahlstrom (2004) reported that
the work of principals and superintendents has an indirect but powerful
impact on student learning and achievement, second only to the quality
of the instruction students receive in their classrooms.

   Elmore (2004) suggests that part of solution to the complexity of
today's educational environment is distributed leadership. He believes
that responsibility for student achievement must be spread across
five groups: board members (enacting policies and giving broad instructional support), district-level leaders (communicating a coherent
vision, setting SMART goals, and managing effectively), principals
(implementing continuous school-improvement processes), research-

based trainers and program experts (applying pedagogy and content), and classroom teachers (implementing standards-based board-adopted curriculum). It would seem that the task of continuous improvement of student achievement is truly too big for any one person or entity to accomplish alone.

RESEARCH

Local Boards of Education—There is little doubt that the role of the school board has never been more difficult. Villegas (2003) has found that stakeholders in some urban cities feel that the traditional school board is not up to the task of leading during these changing times. Board effectiveness can be influenced by confused and ill-defined roles, competing political interests that interfere or distract resources and energy away from improvement issues, increasing voter apathy results in unrepresentative boards, and insufficient and old-fashioned types and levels of information given to them, which is not sufficient for today's school.

As federal and state mandates require increasing public accountability, school-to-school and district-to-district comparisons influence real estate values, and special interest groups demand the fulfillment of their agenda(s)—their roles and responsibilities have become confusing. What is clear is that the need for reform and accountability is not just evident at the classroom, school, and district level. Some are giving control of districts to their mayors, while others are finding it increasingly difficult to obtain individuals to run for open positions. While Villegas' (2003) report focused on urban school boards, the recommendations work for all boards of education, regardless of size. "Districts need policy stability and consistency to make and sustain difficult changes. Context is crucial. Many school boards may require state and federal assistance to strengthen their data infrastructure" (p. 6–7). The need for research in all areas of education is self-evident, but none more so than in the area of school boards' impact on student achievement.

The *Iowa Lighthouse Study* examined the relationship between school boards of education and student achievement. The Iowa School Board Association's *Lighthouse Study* (2000) found that school board members of high-achieving school districts (called *moving*), showed greater understanding and influence in each of the *seven key areas* for school renewal than those districts struggling (called *stuck*). Value was seen in the board receiving training in the following seven areas:

1. Shared leadership
2. Continuous improvement & shared decision-making
3. Ability to create & sustain initiatives
4. Supportive workplace for staff
5. Staff development
6. Support for school sites through data & information
7. Community involvement

Although a causal relationship cannot be determined, the evidence suggests that training and development to support knowledge and understanding in these areas may contribute to student achievement. Districts viewed as moving demonstrated belief systems focused on the possibilities, not the improbabilities. Moving districts held elevated beliefs in the power of:

1. Students viewed as emerging & flexible
2. School's job to release students' potential
3. No excuses!
4. Constant quest for improvement of system

District/Central Office

Fullan (1991) stated, "The district administrator is the single most important individual for setting the expectations and tone of the **pattern of change** within the local district" (p. 191). Fielding, Kerr, and Rosier (2004) reported on Kennewick, Washington, school district's amazing achievements of 95 percent in reading and math. Significant contributors to the improvements were dedicated teachers, staff, and administrators, and the community's dedication to reading improvement. Additionally, unlike most changes of this magnitude, where the orders are given to the media and the building principal to share with the teachers, it is impressive that when the mandate to achieve 95 percent in reading and math (across grade levels) was issued, a member(s) of the school board and superintendent visited each building to talk, answer questions, and listen. This unified front (board of education + superintendent + building principal) made an amazing statement to the district and the community.

Building Level

Current research suggests that exemplary principal leadership is vital to student achievement and that the culture of the school is greatly influenced by building-level leaders. Research by Cotton (2003) identified twenty-five categories of principal behaviors that positively affect student achievement. Exemplary leaders can be recognized. In addition, when appointing principals to schools that need to be turned around and bring about difficult change (second order), specific characteristics need to be considered in the hiring process. New research gives us profound insight into what type of principal will be successful in facilitating second-order change.

Waters, Marzano, and McNulty (2005), in a meta-analysis of the research, found a relationship between leadership and student achievement. The correlation between leadership behavior and student achievement is about $r = 0.25$. Waters, Marzano, and McNulty's research has shown that there are twenty-one specific leadership responsibilities and sixty-six leadership practices that have a significant effect on student achievement:

- Knowledge of curriculum, instruction, assessment ($r = 0.25$)
- Optimizer ($r = 0.20$)
- Intellectual stimulation ($r = 0.24$)
- Change agent ($r = 0.25$)
- Monitors/evaluates ($r = 0.27$)
- Flexibility ($r = 0.28$)
- Ideas/beliefs ($r = 0.22$)
- Culture ($r = 0.25$)
- Communication ($r = 0.23$)
- Order ($r = 0.25$)
- Input ($r = 0.25$)
- Discipline ($r = 0.27$)

- Resource ($r = 0.25$)
- Curriculum, instruction assessment ($r = 0.20$)
- Focus ($r = 0.24$)
- Visibility ($r = 0.20$)
- Contingent rewards ($r = 0.24$)
- Affirmation ($r = 0.19$)
- Outreach ($r = 0.27$)
- Situational awareness ($r = 0.33$)
- Relationship ($r = 0.18$)

Teacher Leadership

The complexities of leading a school today are innumerable. Limiting leadership to just one person (the principal) or a couple of individuals (assistant principals/deans of students) is limiting the potential achievement of every student and adult in that building. Many districts realize the untapped resource of teacher leaders. Districts are also exploring the avenue of teacher leadership by empowering teachers to take greater responsibility for student learning and the culture of the school in general. Teacher leaders are selected at the grade levels in elementary school, at the team level in middle schools, and as chairs of departments at the high school level. Teacher leadership is found in highly effective schools. Teacher empowerment appears to encourage greater collaboration and accountability for student achievement. It encourages input into organizational priorities and focuses on results. Lambert (1998a) has stated,

> School leadership needs to be a broad concept that is separated from person, role, and a discrete set of individual behaviors. It needs to be embedded in the school community as a whole. Such a broadening of the concept of leadership suggest shared responsibility for a shared purpose of community. (p. 5)

Teacher leaders are those individuals who love teaching, who do not want to leave the classroom but have a desire to be part of the solution outside of their classroom. Hirsch (1997) noted these teacher leaders can lead in the following ways: by membership or leadership on the

School-Improvement Team (SIP Team), by serving as department/ team/grade-level chairs, as mentors, as study-group facilitators, as action researchers, as literacy and/or math coaches, as staff developers, and as curriculum writers. All of these roles are crucial to the systemic and continuous improvement of a school or district.

> For this reason, we view teacher leadership less as a magic bullet for quickly solving the "numbers" problem and more as a *critical feature in a coherent and focused set of district policies to address the substantive challenges of reform.* (p. 3)

LEADERSHIP MENTORING FOR ALL

Many states have mandated that districts establish administrative and teacher mentoring programs. Dollars are being authorized, yet no accountability system for program effectiveness is in place. The research (Ingersoll, 2001; Jacob, 2007) is clear that the retention rate is much higher within those districts (rural, urban, suburban) that have quality teacher mentoring programs. Given the negative impact of constant/ high teacher turnover, the need for a high-quality mentoring program is understated.

The politics of teacher mentoring are often at a subliminal level of interference. Sufficient resources are not allocated and little, if any, accountability is conducted. In some cases, there is a distorted belief that "We did just fine without a formal mentor, so anything we do will be better than what we had." This faulty thinking will result in a program being offered, but often not for the right reasons.

Administrators must be cautious when selecting the mentors. The "halo effect" can have devastating results (negatively impacting teacher morale and supporting the sharing of bad practices). Board members should not be involved in the actual selection (as most evaluation opinions would not be based on teacher observation but on "liking the person"). In many cases, the most effective teacher is not necessarily the "most popular" teacher in the building. Unfortunately, administrators will sometimes select mentors based on seniority or likeability factors and not on objective evaluations and achievement data results.

SCHOOL BOARD

School board members are elected or appointed to represent the stake-holders in the community. They are empowered to ask essential questions that will result in continuous improvement for the school district. They are called upon to make crucial decisions that will not only affect the district but the community as well. The community is as strong as its schools, and the schools are as strong as the community desires them to be. School board members are encouraged to solicit community input on decisions and to keep the community informed of the progress the district is making in garnering the best education for all students enrolled.

Research suggests that effective school boards model shared leadership and demonstrate their ability to create and sustain initiatives in the district. Successful school boards seek to provide a supportive working environment for all employees and are actively involved in examining data and information on the schools and the district as a whole. Exemplary school board members want the best possible education for all students in the district and work collaboratively with administrators and teachers to establish priorities and resources to make this possible. School board members need training to keep abreast with how to effectively work with members of the community and school administrators to bring about needed changes and celebrations in the district.

Fundamental to continuous improvement is a board of education that exemplifies mature conduct, effectively communicates (listening as much as talking), and demonstrates a dedication to every child (including the poor, the minority, the non-English-speaking student, the gifted and talented, and the dropout).

QUESTIONS THAT SUPPORT CONTINUOUS IMPROVEMENT

1. The most common question asked when a new program or project is requested should be: "What evidence can be provided that the money we have spent has accomplished (your goal)?"
2. What evidence exists that the current administrative evaluation system is supportive and goal-oriented toward student achievement?

3. How effective is the current evaluation instrument? Is it standards-based and tied to the research?
4. Are coaching and feedback provided to leaders to enhance their performance?
5. Is formal mentoring provided for newly appointed principals and principals at risk?
6. Do we have the *best* people in leadership? Finish the following sentence: "I believe we have the best leaders because they _____."
7. How should program decisions in the district be made to enhance the effectiveness of student achievement?
8. What are the *essential questions* that should be addressed regarding student achievement and student support services in our district?
9. What types of advisory councils do you have in place? What level of involvement do your students have on these councils?

School Board

1. How often does the school board seek advice from the state association and National School Boards Association to increase their effectiveness?
2. How do we self-evaluate the line between shared leadership and micromanaging?
3. How often does the school board conduct a "self evaluation" and share it with the community stakeholders? Is the "self evaluation" followed by a plan of action for improvement?
4. How can school board members be assured of the effectiveness of teachers, administrators, and support personnel?
5. How can school board members be assured that the district priority of continuous improvement is actualized on a day-to-day basis?
6. What data do we have that supports expenditures for school board training and attendance at school board conferences?
7. How does this investment of time and money result in more efficient board decisions and positively impact student achievement?

8. Every school day reflects an expenditure of time, effort, energy, and money—what evidence will you provide your community that this was a good investment?

9. How do you evaluate the superintendent?

10. How do you handle complaints and/or controversy? (The change process research indicates that people will be unhappy, and unhappy people will complain. It is feathering out the legitimate complainers from the whiners. Boards cannot ask for change to happen and not support the leadership that is attempting to make it happen.)

11. How much do you model the types of behaviors that you expect from the students in the district and your building and district-level leadership?

Superintendents and Other Central Office Personnel

12. What data do we have that our expenditures for the central office (superintendent and, when applicable, the directors of curriculum and instruction, transportation, budgeting, grants, public relations, etc.) are making a difference in the district culture and academic achievement of students K-12?

13. What data do we have that the building-level administrators are being given the level of technical support needed to perform their jobs?

14. What does the data reflect regarding principal performance and student achievement?

15. How are administrators monitored, supported, and developed to continuously improve?

16. How are aspiring administrators identified? Mentored? Trained?

17. How often does the central office examine data sets? How often do discussions of data sets occur?

18. What types of professional development has the central office received? What is the evidence of the utilization of the training? How was the information shared with other administrators, the board, and teachers?

19. What has been done to find new resources for meeting program needs?

Principal

20. What data do we have that our expenditures for leadership (principal, assistant principals, deans, department chairs, team leaders, guidance directors, teacher leaders) are making a difference in the school culture and academic achievement of students K-12?

21. What leadership training exists for principals, assistant principals, deans, department chairs, team leaders, guidance directors, grade-level teacher leaders, and other leaders in the school district?

22. What has been done to find new resources for meeting program needs?

23. How are formative observations and summative evaluations carried out? What impact do they have upon teaching and learning?

24. Do all of your teachers receive evaluation ratings of "excellent" or "superior"? If so, why?

25. How much time do you spend in classrooms?

26. How much time do you spend with parents? What types of parent involvement and parent-support programs does your school offer? What impact do they have?

Teacher Leadership

27. How much time is allotted for the effective utilization of teachers leadership knowledge and skills?

28. How many teachers received instructional coaching during the semester?

29. How are teacher leaders were selected? Is there a rigorous system in place or is it connected to seniority?

30. What evidence can you provide that your district or school could benefit from a teacher–leader program?

31. What types of action research might you expect from your teacher leaders? Who would determine the project? How would the project be funded, evaluated, and reported?

32. What data do we have that shows how expenditures for our first- and second-year teacher mentoring programs are making a difference in teacher effectiveness and students' academic achievement?

33. What criteria are used in the selection of mentors?

34. How is data used to evaluate the program's effectiveness?
35. What is the perception of the first- and second-year teachers in terms of the program's effectiveness?
36. What are the principals' and mentors' perceptions of the program's effectiveness?
37. What celebrations exist for the growth and development of both mentors and mentees?
38. How aligned are the outcomes to the teacher-evaluation system? What is the principal's role in the process?
39. What is the district rate of retention of new teachers?

DATA SETS THAT COULD BE REPORTED

School Board

1. Attendance of every board member at all school board meetings.
2. Attendance of every board member at committee meetings.
3. Punctuality of every school board member at every board and committee meeting.
4. Attendance at some level of training for board members (local, regional, state, and/or national).
5. Does the school board conduct a scheduled (annually, every other year, or every three years) self-audit, publish the results, and benchmark SMART goals for their continuous improvement as a board?
6. How much time is spent at board meetings discussing topics that directly impact academics and programs (such as the arts, support services, etc.)?
7. How much time is spent at school board meetings discussing student achievement?
8. How effectively has the board hired school leaders? In reviewing the past record of superintendents, how many have had a positive impact on student learning and achievement?
9. How comprehensively does the board tie its interviewing process and questions to the current needs of the district, current initiatives, and future goals?

10. How does the board evaluate the superintendent? Is part of the evaluation tied to student performance? Administrator performance? Improved district culture and climate? What mechanism is in place for succession planning? Continuity of leadership is important, especially in the middle of an improvement initiative.

Superintendent and Central Office

11. How often does the superintendent gather data from his/her administrators, teachers, and parents related to their performance? What is done with these data?
12. How many new resources were brought into the district last year? What program-evaluation component was put into place with the new funds ensuring effective use and fiscal responsibility?
13. What is the culture and climate of the district? How does it compare to previous scores?
14. How is job performance tied to data?

Principal and Building-Level Leadership

15. Keep a log of principal involvement with the teachers that asks, "How many times did the principal 'help me?' How often was my principal in my room, offering instructional leadership?"
16. How many parent involvement and parent-support activities were held within the building? Provide evidence that all subgroups are represented in your attempt to involve parents.
17. What evidence of sustained and research-based professional-development planning and implementation were provided?
18. Was a comprehensive professional-development plan and schedule turned into the central office by May 1st? Was an evaluation component part of the plan? How will you know your investment results in improved teaching and learning?
19. How many coaching or modeling sessions did teacher leaders report?
20. How were teacher leaders evaluated for this component of their performance?

SUMMARY

Leaders have known, since *A Nation at Risk* was reported in 1983, that the quality of educational leadership is paramount to effective schools. All levels of impact must be evaluated for effectiveness, not just those that affect students. From the board of education and administrators, whose unified actions toward a quality education for all, to the teacher leaders within every building, individuals must work smarter, not harder. Leadership must ask tough questions and be prepared to answer tough questions. Communities must expect and support the training of school board members, administrators, and teacher leaders. They must also expect results from their investments in those trainings. Leadership must focus on an all-inclusive model for input and decision-making. Individuals from students, parents, community members, teachers, support staff, policy makers, and legislators must have voices that are heard when major initiatives are undertaken. Although the ultimate decisions are those of the board of education, we cannot say it is a public school and minimize the public's voice, role, and responsibilities—not if we want local school control to remain a staple of American democracy.

Resources for Continued Exploration

National School Boards Association: Key Works of School Boards. A Meta-analysis of 30 Years of Research on Leadership and Student Achievement. http://www.mcrel.org

What Works in Schools: Translating Research into Action by Robert Marzano. http://www.ASCD.org

Value-Added Assessment of Teachers by Haggai Kupermintz. The Tennessee Value-Added Assessment System (TVAAS)—statistical methodology to estimate the aggregated yearly growth in student learning, as reflected in changes in test scores in five tested academic subjects (http://www.asu.edu/educ/epsl/EPRU/documents/EPRU%202002-101/Chapter%2011-Kupermintz-Final.htm).

The Organizational Climate Description Questionnaire (OCDQ), for all levels (http://www.coe.ohio-state.edu/whoy).

Leading for Learning: Reflective Tools for School and District Leaders. (February 2003). University of Washington: Center for the Study of Teaching and Policy. http://depts.washington.edu/ctpmail/PDFs/LforLSummary-02-03.pdf

ⓑ

TEACHER, PRINCIPAL, AND SUPERINTENDENT SHORTAGES—WILL ANYBODY DO?

When the infrastructure shifts, everything rumbles.

Stan Davis

The essence of effectiveness is achieving the results you want in a way that enables you to get even more of these results in the future.

Stephen Covey

ESSENTIAL QUESTIONS

Is there a shortage of well-qualified teachers, principals, and superintendents to lead schools and districts?

If shortages exist, what are the specific reasons for the shortages?

How will we advance the educational reform agenda in public schools if there are barriers to finding and retaining well-qualified teachers, principals, and superintendents?

The prevailing thinking in this country is that there is an insufficient pool of qualified teachers, principals, and superintendents. There is a perception that our colleges and universities are not training enough of these individuals to meet current and future demands.

RESEARCH

Teachers

Ingersoll (2003) addressed the teacher shortage challenge by asking this essential question: "Is there really a teacher shortage?" He asserted that even though the demand for more teachers had increased, the data do not indicate a shortage.

Current data suggest that school staffing problems are not solely or even primarily caused by teacher shortfalls resulting from increases either in student enrollment or in teacher retirement. In contrast, the data suggest that school staffing problems are to a large extent a result of a "revolving door"—where large numbers of teachers leave the profession for reasons other than retirement.

Many school districts across the country are designing and increasing their teacher recruitment programs without looking at the etiology of the problem—high teacher turnover. Very few studies have looked at the organizational culture of the district or specific schools to examine the effects of the organizational culture on teacher attrition. Ingersoll (2001) studied teacher turnover as an organizational phenomenon. He examined the role of school characteristics and organizational conditions. The data showed that low salaries, the lack of school administrator support, student discipline problems, and limited faculty input into decision-making contributed to the high turnover rates. Ingersoll (2001) asserted that teacher recruitment programs alone would not solve the problem if schools and districts did not address organizational culture and teacher retention.

In the past decade, districts have been instituting teacher-mentoring programs to support beginning teachers. The financial expenditures of this effort along with teacher recruitment can be costly, and many times the effectiveness of these programs is never evaluated. In a recent policy brief (American Association of State Colleges and Universities, 2005), the document stated that,

> teacher shortages are less a function of how many teachers are produced than of how many are lost each year through turnover and early attrition. This "revolving door" problem inflates the "demand" side of the equation and keeps school districts in a perpetual state of intense hiring pressure. (para. 11)

The financial expenditures involved in replacing teachers as well as the impact on student achievement should be topics of discussion at executive staff meetings and school board meetings.

According to Ingersoll's research, "forty-two percent of all departing teachers report as a reason either job dissatisfaction or the desire to pursue a better job, another career, or to improve career opportunities in or out of education" (p. 22). Shortages may be due to the culture of the district and schools and the way the district as a whole values and supports new teachers as well as veteran teachers. Ingersoll (2003) recommended several solutions: better salaries, better student discipline, smaller class sizes, more faculty authority, less paperwork, more opportunities for advancement, reduced workload, more parental involvement, better classroom resources, higher academic standards, mentoring of newcomers, and merit pay.

The American Association of State Colleges and Universities (2005) reported that the United States is *not* facing a teacher shortage. The Association contends that the biggest challenge is the misalignment between supply and demand. In the high-demand fields, and in the western and southeastern states as well as in urban districts with many low-income and minority students, teacher shortages have become a challenge. Clark County School District in Las Vegas, Nevada, began the school year in 2006 with 344 teaching vacancies (nvrjsc1, 2006). Statistics provided by this Association stated that only 60 percent of those trained to be teachers moved directly into teaching, and only 50 to 60 percent would still be teaching in five years (American Association of State Colleges and Universities, 2005).

The National Commission on Teaching and America's Future (2002) stated that we are focusing on the symptom rather than the problem of teacher shortages. They claimed that the shortage is just the visible side of the coin and that the underlying problem is the high attrition rates. They alleged that the question that needs to be asked is, "How do we get the good teachers we have recruited, trained and hired to stay in their jobs" (p. 3)?

Principals

Tucher and Tschannen-Moran (2002) reported that "the graying of school administrators coupled with increased job complexity, rising standards, and greater accountability have led to increased numbers of administrative vacancies national wide" (p. 10). They acknowledged that the number of individuals holding administrative credentials exceeds the number of vacancies, yet they purported that recruitment and retention of administrators is a national challenge. The challenge appears to be the long hours, increased job responsibilities and accountability, and the fact that fewer teachers are selecting administration as a career option.

A 2003 Rand study (Gates et al., 2003) purported that the number of school administrators appeared to be stable but that the profession is aging. The study revealed that school districts are much less likely to hire people under forty and that the new principals will spend fewer years in the positions since most are not likely to remain in the job after fifty-five years of age. The study also indicated that principals were not fleeing schools that served disadvantaged students. The study reported no evidence of a nationwide crisis regarding principal shortages, but acknowledged the differences in states and local school districts. The report recommended that a detailed state-level analysis be conducted on the careers of school administrators. Through this analysis, a greater understanding would be obtained that would benefit the state and local school district.

The 1998 study conducted by National Association of Elementary School Principals (NAESP) and the National Association of Secondary School Principals (NASSP) stated that almost half of the school districts reported a shortage of K-12 principal positions. The study found that principals were retiring at an average age of fifty-seven and that more than one-half planned to retire as soon as they were eligible, which would yield a 40 percent turnover rate in the next decade. In a NAESP (National Association of Elementary School Principals, n. d.) survey conducted in 2000, members indicated that 66 percent would retire within the next six to ten years. The study quoted the U.S. Bureau of Labor Statistics (BLS), which reported that there would be a 13-percent increase in job openings for educational administrators between 2000–2010 and projected that a large number of administrators would retire within the decade.

A survey conducted by the Association of California School Administrators in 2001 found that 90 percent of the districts reported shortages of high school principal candidates, and 73 percent had shortages at the elementary level. At this time, however, the California credentialing agency had 34,000 individuals on file with administrative credentials, which was 11,000 more than was needed to fill the 23,000 positions (Bell, 2001).

Howley and Pendarvis (2003) claimed that a shortage of qualified candidates does exist in rural districts, especially at the secondary level. The authors asserted that the job pressure, long hours, special programs, collaboration, as well as increased federal and state accountability have added to these pressures. Whitaker (2001) reported in her study of more than 100 superintendents that 50 percent reported a "somewhat extreme" or "extreme" shortage of principal candidates. "Given that 90 percent of the respondents indicated a moderate to extreme shortage of principal candidates, the issue appears to deserve attention" (p. 84).

Roza (2003) found that the average district receives seventeen applicants for each principal's position, which was a decline of approximately two applicants per position over a seven-year period. Human resource directors reported little difficulty filling principal positions. The study concluded that:

> despite widespread publicity about a universal shortage of principals, "shortages" are not the norm. Where there have been reductions in the number of qualified candidates, these conditions are district and even school-specific and more pronounced at the secondary level than the elementary level. In addition, perceptions of the "shortage" are driven by a new and different kind of school principal. (p. 1)

Roza (2003) also reported that some districts are avoided by principal candidates. These districts are earmarked with poverty, large minority populations, and lower salaries. Rose asserts that this is what separates the high-need districts and schools from the low-need in terms of shortages. The other dilemma that this research revealed is the fact that there is a discrepancy between what superintendents perceive they want in a principal and the experiences human resources personnel rely on to screen and hire candidates. The findings indicated that many times the human resources department asserted they wanted people with leadership skills and then defaulted to the traditional qualifications. The study also found that new principal hires have an average of fourteen years of teaching experience and, while the human resource department is satisfied with the new hires, "the superintendents continued to express dissatisfaction about inadequate leadership abilities of the new principals" (p. 2). Recommendations from this study were: (1) get the incentives right; (2) hiring criteria should be aligned with the knowledge, skills, and experience the superintendent seeks; (3) redefine the principal position (p. 3)

Superintendents

Buchanan (2004) reported that eleven of the nation's largest districts have spent time and resources searching for new superintendents. These districts include Miami-Dade in Florida; the three largest districts in Texas; and districts in Washington, DC; St. Louis, MO; Portland, OR; Minneapolis, MN; and Tucson, AZ. Buchanan (2004) also reported that a study conducted in 2003 by the University of Washington revealed that 90 percent of the superintendents in the 100 largest districts perceived that they needed more power to hire and fire, reconfigure schools, and make changes in the curriculum. The dilemma for superintendents included no shortage of critics, the ever-present need to analyze the politics and navigate the land mines, astute public relations skills, and constant preparation for and attention from the media. Glass, Bjork, and Brunner (2000) stated,

> Preparing the next generation of superintendents, however, must include ways to extend thinking beyond "doing administration" to "knowing why" they are doing it and effectively communicating that purpose to others. In addition, it is becoming evident that an increasing number of superintendents are viewing the position as "impossible," and the salary and benefits as inadequate, contributing to many highly qualified professionals deciding not to enter candidate pools. (p. 161)

QUESTIONS FOR REFLECTION AND DISCUSSION

Teacher

   1. What are the statistics/data on teacher retention for this district?

2. What does the data reveal on the organizational culture within this district and schools?

3. What does the aggregated data acquired during exit interviews reveal about reasons people are leaving? What process is used for exit interviews of faculty and support staff? Who synthesizes the data and how is it used for improvement? To whom are the data reported?

4. How are we using the data to improve teacher retention? What changes can be identified as a result of data?

5. How effectively are we evaluating our teacher recruitment initiatives?

6. How effectively are we evaluating our teacher mentoring program? What data can be presented that teacher mentoring is making a difference in teacher retention?

7. What process exists that recognizes outstanding teaching in the schools?

8. What structure does this district support for teachers to acquire leadership roles (for example, grade-level chairs, team leaders at the middle schools, department or division chairs)?

9. If your district is a small rural district, what specific plans exist for recruiting teachers? (The research indicates that attraction for young couples is high related to quality-of-living issues. Short commutes, security, lower costs of living, and a perception of being "family-oriented" can all be attractive incentives for relocating to the country. Using classroom teachers, rather than brochures or principals, to share these strengths with perspective candidates has proven to work for some districts).

Principals

10. What data do we have on the retention of exemplary, "walk on water" principals? (These individuals may not be the most "liked" because they have initiated *accountability* and expected *results*.)

11. What results can be reported about the effectiveness of principal mentoring?

12. What opportunities are supported by the district for principal networking?

13. What opportunities are supported by the district for professional development? For opportunities to think, grow, and do more than survive the job?

14. What process exists that recognizes outstanding leadership in the schools?

Superintendents

15. How can you ensure that the individual hired as superintendent is an intellectual, emotional, moral, and philosophical match to the district's needs and the community (retention is directly related to this match)?

16. What support systems exist?

17. What process exists that recognizes outstanding leadership by the superintendent?

DATA SETS THAT COULD BE REPORTED

1. What are the projected faculty openings, due to retirements, for the next five years?

2. How many external applications are received for job postings (pareducators, certified, support staff, administrative)?

3. How many contract rejections are experienced by the district when jobs are offered?

4. What is the school culture and organizational health of each building? How does this impact new teachers and/or teacher recruitment?

5. What reputation does the district have for hiring and retaining new teachers?

6. What is the district culture and organizational health?

7. What is the status of our substitute teacher pool?

8. How many paraeducators do we have who have a desire to teach someday?

9. How many hours of mentoring do new teachers receive? How is the quality monitored?

10. How many hours of mentoring do new administrators receive? How is the quality monitored?

11. What is the synthesis of the exit interview data sets?

SUMMARY

The question remains whether the United States indeed has a teacher, principal, and superintendent shortage or whether it is more accurately a systems error. The data reported that there are a sufficient number of certified administrators meeting the nation's leadership openings. And although shortages exist in certain teaching areas (i.e., math, science, special education, foreign languages, and bilingual), the systems error is less about recruitment and salary and more about how individuals are supported and mentored once employed. The organizational culture of isolation and resistance to continuous improvement are also variables that result in talented individuals leaving our classrooms.

Teacher- and leadership-preparation programs also have some responsibility in the retention dilemma. Recent scathing reports have noted that too little emphasis has been placed on modeling research-based practices in the halls of academia. While an underlying battle quietly grows, are universities institutions that develop well-rounded citizens, or are they training institutes? No educator would dispute the complexities of their job today—continually growing curricula, changing definitions of family, high-stakes testing, lagging computer technology, poverty, increasing numbers of students with little to no English skills, and student apathy and anger. Yet in too many teacher-preparation programs, classroom management is not a required class. Students spend time in general elective courses with no direct relationship to the knowledge and skills they will need to effectively teach. There are no easy answers. Each partner (the school, the district, higher education, individual departments, and grade levels) in the equation must step back and examine their role in the high dropout rate of teachers—and do something about it.

RESOURCES FOR CONTINUED EXPLORATION

American Association of School Administrators. http://www.aasa.org
National School Boards Association. http://www.nsba.org/site/index.asp

14

PARAPROFESSIONALS/TEACHER ASSISTANTS—MEMBERS OF THE TEAM, NOT SUBSTITUTES

Keep your dreams alive.
Understand to achieve anything requires faith and belief in yourself,
vision, hard work, determination, and dedication.
Remember all things are possible for those who believe.

Gail Devers

ESSENTIAL QUESTION

What are the roles, relationships, and responsibilities of school-based paraprofessionals in the education of our children?

DEFINITIONS

Paraeducator/paraprofessional (para): A term coined by Pickett in 1989 with the National Resource Center for Paraprofessionals (NRCP) identifying those who work alongside teachers. These individuals are sometimes referred to as a paraprofessional, teacher's aide, teacher's associate, teacher's assistant, education technician, transition trainer/job coach, home visitor, and/or classroom aide (Pickett, 2002). There is no federal definition for an aide, thus it is recommended that the term not be used.

No Child Left Behind Act (NCLB): According to NCLB Act of 2001, all paraprofessionals shall have:

(A) completed at least 2 years of study at an institution of higher education;

(B) obtained an associate's (or higher) degree;

(C) met a rigorous standard of quality and can demonstrate, through a formal State or local academic assessment—

    (i) knowledge of, and the ability to assist in instructing, reading, writing, and mathematics; or

    (ii) knowledge or, and the ability to assist in instructing, reading readiness, writing readiness, and mathematics readiness, as appropriate. (20 U.S.C. § 6319[c]); *No Child Left Behind*, p. 200)

The National Center for Education Statistics (Snyder & Hoffman, 2001) reported a 48-percent increase in instructional paraprofessionals (paras) in the United States between 1990 and 1998. The National Resource Center for Paraprofessionals (NRCP), in a 2001 survey, reported the equivalent of about 525,000 full-time paras worked in U.S. schools. Some unsubstantiated claims state that there are a million paras working in the United States. More than half of the paras are employed in special-education classrooms as one-on-one student assistants. Title-1 programs or multilingual classrooms employ about 130,000 paras. Paras working in early childhood education settings, libraries, media centers, and computer labs make up approximately 100,000. Government economists expect jobs for teacher assistants to grow as fast as the average for all occupations through 2014. Areas where population and school enrollments are growing most quickly, such as many communities in the South and West, should continue to have a strong need for teacher assistants (U.S. Bureau of Labor Statistics, 2006).

Paras have shared in the development of public schools for the past fifty years. Their roles and responsibilities have over time become less clerical and more instructionally focused (Pickett, 2002). Reducing the adult-to-student ratio in a classroom through the use of paraeducators is a common collective bargaining issue. In many districts, however, their roles, relationships, and responsibilities are not clearly defined (Ashbaker & Morgan, 2000–2001; Gerber, Finn, Archilles, & Boyd-Zaharias, 2001), and thus neither is their impact.

The issue is not whether to employ paraprofessionals but rather whether they are used effectively. Usually, little attention is given to their impact on student learning and achievement. Hard questions, discussions, and evaluations need to take place in order to ensure positive student outcomes. This chapter will examine the research behind the effective use of paras. Districts will be asked to compare their usage and belief systems to what the research says should be happening.

If the district's reason to employ paras is to aid in student supervision or to reduce teacher busywork by employing people to cut, color, or hang bulletin boards, then accountability beyond attendance, professional conduct, and collegial attitudes should not be expected. If, however, any part of the reason for employing paras is related to an expectation for improved student achievement, then additional accountability indicators must be reported. Quality performance is closely tied to quality professional development, supervising teacher relationships (Marks, Schrader, & Levine, 1999), expectations, and job descriptions. Even with NCLB's requirement for an associate's degree (in anything), paras may have much to learn before being "ready" for classroom work. "A test passer is not a bad thing. . . . But it may not give us what want in terms of effective people in the classroom" (Hardy, 2004, p. 33).

Allen (2002) reported that most teachers don't know how to use paras. Putting two or three adults together in the same space doesn't mean that they will know how to work together. French (2007) found 56.8 percent of paraeducators were supervised by teachers with no preparation to supervise. Of these, 61.1 percent, once on the job, received little to no supervision. This lack of training in supervision can cause relational problems between supervising teachers and their paras. Key to the retention of quality paraeducators is the process of job assignment and the consideration of personalities, interests, and required job skills.

The research on the impact of paras related to student achievement describes mixed results. Gerber, Finn, Achilles, and Boyd-Zaharias (2001) reported that in the first and second grades the extent to which aides performed administrative, instructional, and noninstructional tasks was not related to any measure of student achievement. In grade 3, classes with paras, who spent a medium amount of time on instructional tasks, showed minimum advantages on some measures of mathematics and reading. In general, their research found achievement in classrooms with a paraprofessional was no higher than that in a regular classroom with no aide (Gerber, Finn, Achilles, & Boyd-Zaharias, 2001; Giangreco, Broer, & Edelman, 2001; Jones & Bender, 1993). In fact, students in smaller classrooms outperformed those in classrooms with paras in every instance. The State of Tennessee's Student/Teacher Achievement Ratio study of grades K-3 (Word, Johnston, Bain, & Fulton, 1990) reported that, although being in a classroom with a para may increase reading scores in first and second grade, these results were sporadic. There are greater benefits to having smaller class sizes.

A 1995 study (Salzberg & Morgan) suggested that paras may feel a greater sense of responsibility for their special-education students than the regular division teacher. Giangreco (2003) reported that the single most important contributor to a special education student's success in the regular classroom was the level of that teacher's engagement. Granger and Grek (2005) reported that paras could make significant differences in increasing student literacy skills if they: (a) had been trained on phonemic awareness, alphabetic decoding, and spelling; (b) demonstrated warmth and enthusiasm toward all students; and (c) used explicit scientifically based methods.

Archilles, Finn, Gerber, and Boyd (2000) found that paras spend their time:

- 40 percent on administrative tasks
- 25–30 percent on instructional tasks
- 20–25 percent on noninstructional interaction with teachers

Additional benefits to the local school and/or classroom focus on more qualitative aspects of learning. Paras are local, long-standing members of the neighborhood and/or community and thus know the local history, families, and oftentimes the students (Sturm, 2004). This has proven to sometimes have political ramifications. Terminating the employment of a local para, well-known and well-liked but ineffective and/or inefficient, can sometimes result in lengthy legal battles as well as a disruption for the school, district, and community. On the positive side, having paras with strong local ties who are invested in the school and the community and see the students in their neighborhoods, local stores, and in church creates a strong bond. These relationships create strong personal connections to parents and caregivers. This strong bond can allow the school to function as an extended family, benefiting the student.

Common Concerns and Issues

1. In most districts or buildings, paraeducators do not receive an orientation or entry-level training to their new job (Ghere & York-Barr, 2003; Giangreco, Broer, & Edelman, 2003).
2. Clearly defined job descriptions aligned to each position are needed. Additionally, matching individual requisite skills and competencies to the position and to the classroom teacher and/or student would facilitate increased performance and improved outcomes.
3. Professional-development training should be provided in teaming, discipline, and communication between the paraeducator and the regular classroom teacher. French (1998) found a need for training in behavior management and instructional cues. Giangreco, Broer, and Edelman (2003) reported a need for on-the-job training to match responsibilities. Since the passage of NCLB there has been a decrease in the number of paras providing unsupervised instructional support down from 47 percent to 36 percent (American Federation of Teachers, 2006).
4. Generally, special-education paraeducators are included in the same training as classroom teachers or not given any training at all (Downing, Ryndak, & Clark, 2000). Conventional wisdom would indicate a strong need for quality professional development in areas outside of content and classroom management (French, 2007). If certified, bachelor-degreed teachers need continuous improvement, what would be the reason not to provide quality training to those with an associate's degree or less? The one-size-fits-all training program is no more effective for paras than it was for certified teachers or students.

QUESTIONS FOR REFLECTION AND DISCUSSION

1. How are paraeducators being used in your classrooms (analysis of time spent in instructional work with students and schedules)?

2. How well do written job descriptions actually describe the specific tasks assigned to the paraeducators? Will a generic, one-size-fits-all job description work for all paraeducators in your district/building? (Consider the differences between the paras assigned to Title I, regular classrooms, one-on-one special-education (such as for the blind, quadriplegic, autistic) resource, library media, playground/lunch room—would one job description fit all of these different tasks?)

3. What type of orientation and mentoring are paraeducators given?

4. What is the screening process for hiring and assigning paraeducators to students and/or teachers? Are personalities, skills, and other variables given consideration when the assignment is made?

5. How are paraeducators evaluated? Who is involved?

   a. Is this evaluation tied to effectiveness, standards, curricular knowledge, and student outcomes?

   b. Is there a summative feedback process? Is it formal or informal?

   c. What type(s) of formative (ongoing) feedback is shared with the paraeducator(s)? How is this monitored? Documented?

6. How much time do you spend discussing paraeducators' impact on learning? Or is the majority of the discussion focused around collective bargaining agreements, budget issues, and/or class size?

7. What professional development is scheduled for paraeducators?

8. How often are paraeducators included in the training that the teachers receive? If not, why not? If they are, what type of formal follow-up is expected? Who does the follow-up? If classroom teachers are expected to complete the follow-up observations, are they trained in doing so?

9. How often are paraeducators surveyed for their perception of the school culture, climate, effectiveness of their utilization, etc.?

How are these perceptions shared with stakeholders, and how are they used for continuous improvement?

10. How are paraeducators recognized within your district/school? What title is given to the position—aide, associate, para, paraeducator, paraprofessional? What recognitions exist to honor the work that they do? (Ashbaker & Morgan, 2000–2001; Gerber et al., 2001; Shellard, 2002)

DATA SETS THAT COULD BE REPORTED

1. _____ Number of minutes and/or hours of direct instructional contact with students (tutoring, listening to read, reading aloud to the student(s), assisting with schoolwork, etc., versus putting up bulletin boards, running the copy machine, etc.)?

2. _____ Number of full days that paraeducators substitute "taught" in a classroom?

3. _____ Number of partial days that paraeducators substitute "taught" in a classroom?

4. _____ Number of paraeducators who are certified teachers?

5. _____ Number of one-on-one (paraeducators to special-education student) satisfaction surveys completed by family/student?

6. _____ Observational data indicating special-education student(s) progress toward independence (conscious attempts to not foster dependency)?

7. _____ Survey data related to paraeducators' self-perception of the job, performance, impact, program quality, strengths, and concerns?

8. _____ Survey data related to teachers' perception of the paraeducator's job performance, impact, program quality, strengths, and concerns?

SUMMARY

In many districts, paraprofessionals are embedded into the teacher's collective bargaining agreement. In these cases, their presence will continue. In every classroom that has a paraeducator(s), the teacher, the administrator, and the para need to sit down and evaluate effectiveness and impact. In many cases, the para will have many good ideas for the continuous improvement of the classroom, school, and district. In addition, he/she may have some strong recommendations for the development of their own professional growth.

Paraeducators need quality orientation, mentoring, and continuous training—just as all members of the team for continuous improvement do. It should be noted that the majority of the research found focused on primary (K-3) grade levels. It is therefore imperative that additional research be conducted on the following areas: paras impact on students' academic, social, and emotional growth and development during all ages/grade levels.

RESOURCES FOR CONTINUED EXPLORATION

National Resource Center for Paraprofessionals. http://www.nrcpara.org/
The PARAprofessional Resource and Research Center. http://www.paracenter
.org/PARACenter/
The American Federation of Teachers. http://www.aft.org/psrp/
Center for Disability and Community Inclusion at the University of Vermont.
http://www.uvm.edu/~cdci/paraprep/
Doyle, M. B. (2002). *The paraprofessional's guide to the inclusive classroom:
Working as a team.* Baltimore, MD: Brookes.

CAREER AND TECHNICAL EDUCATION—PREPARATION FOR THE REAL WORLD

New technology, globalization and the rising power of international brands are changing the way we work and fueling the competition for talent.

J. Winter & C. Jackson

ESSENTIAL QUESTION

What impact does the career and technical education program have on the students who are enrolled in career and technical education courses in this district?

DEFINITIONS

Career and Technical Education/Vocational Education (**CTE**)—CTE includes a sequence of courses or a program of study that affords students the opportunity to acquire the knowledge and skills for successful career entry or postsecondary education.

Career Academies—Academies are located within a school, at a designated center, or at a worksite and have a career focus, such as the health sciences. The curriculum includes integration of academic core content (math, science, English, social studies) into the career and technical curriculum. The academy provides students with the knowledge, job skills, and employer involvement through work-study and internships to facilitate entry into the working world or to attend postsecondary education.

Tech Prep—Federal legislation describes a Tech Prep program as a combined secondary and postsecondary program that leads to a specific postsecondary educational outcome and provides vocational/ technical preparation in one or more specific occupational fields (agriculture, business and marketing, health, family and consumer sciences, or industrial occupations). Student competence is built through applied academics in mathematics, science, and communications by a sequential course of study. This leads to placement in employment.

The twenty-first century demands highly skilled and well-educated workers who are able to compete in an international labor market. Our country will need to produce workers who can not only participate actively in a democracy but who also have acquired the knowledge and skills to work effectively in a competitive global economy.

The federal government, through legislation, has played a major role in the establishment and support for career and technical education. This began with the Smith-Hughes Act of 1917, where the major focus was on designing and implementing curricula to meet the needs of the labor force. According to Rojewski (2002) "the passage of the Vocation Education Act of 1963 (PL 88-210) signified a major change in federal policy and direction for career and technical education from an exclusive focus on job preparation to a shared purpose of meeting economic demands that also included a social component" (p. 7). The social component focused on including all students with accessibility for special needs students.

Rojewski (2002) also noted "legislation that followed in 1998 and 2002, reaffirmed a commitment to integrate academic and vocational education, special populations, tech prep (extensive articulation between secondary and post secondary programs), accountability, and expanded the use of technology" (p. 3). The most recent legislation, the

2006 reauthorization of the Perkins Act, replaced the term *vocational education* with *career and technical education*. This reauthorization has put emphasis on high-demand, high-wage, and high-skills occupations. Fundamental changes made by Senate Bill 250 (passed July 11, 2006) to the Perkins Act came in the area of accountability. Focus was placed on the academic achievement of career and technical education students, alignment and coordination between high school and postsecondary institutions, and on improved accountability for the state and local school districts.

RESEARCH

Research on the impact of career and technical education has demonstrated mixed results. Elliott & Zimmerman (2002) compared standardized achievement scores between career and technical education and noncareer and technical education students. They controlled for learning styles, special population, gender, race, and ethnicity. This study reported the need to take a more in-depth look at the data on CTE since the five special population areas (handicapped, limited English proficiency, economically disadvantage, academically disadvantage, and single parent) were significantly associated with lower test scores and were predominately found in the CTE population. (Elliott & Zimmerman, 2002). According to Elliott and Zimmerman,

> The conclusions are simple: Career and technical education students, for the most part, will always do worse on raw score comparisons. When the appropriate extraneous variables are built into the equation and controlled for, there usually is no difference between CTE and other students on standardized test scores. The raw score comparisons are inappropriate because the groups are different. The differences in scores can be attributed to the effects of the extraneous variable and not because of curriculum choices. (pp. 13–14)

Additional findings that have K-12 implications for school districts included the fact that CTE students scored higher in the kinesthetic learning styles category, which was significantly associated with lower test scores. "Black, Hispanic or other males were associated with lower test scores. Hispanic females were associated with lower test scores" (p. 3).

The most comprehensive research on career and technical education was a study mandated by the federal government and conducted by the U.S. Office of Education entitled National Assessment of Vocational Education (NAVE). Key findings from this 2004 study included:

- Students designated as "occupational concentrators" (students enrolled in CTE classes) made substantial gains on the National Assessment of Educational Progress (NAEP) twelfth-grade test scores versus "non-concentrators" (students not enrolled in CTE classes). See Chart 15.1.
- Secondary students who participated in vocational programs have increased their academic course taking and achievement (Chart 15.2).
- Participation in vocational courses positively impacts students' future earnings (Chart 15.3).

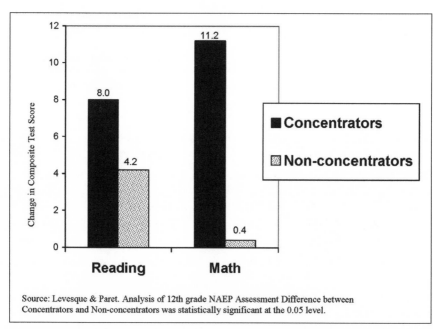

Source: Levesque & Paret. Analysis of 12th grade NAEP Assessment Difference between Concentrators and Non-concentrators was statistically significant at the 0.05 level.

Chart 15.1. Change in NAEP Twelfth-Grade Test Scores for Concentrators and Non-concentrators: Reading 1994–1998 and Mathematics 1990–2000.

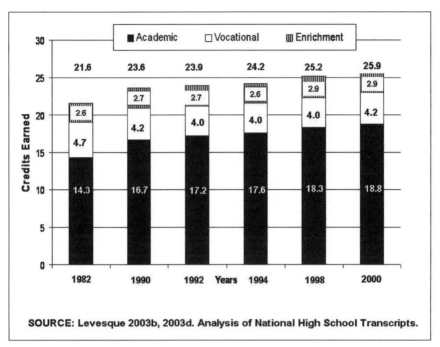

SOURCE: Levesque 2003b, 2003d. Analysis of National High School Transcripts.

Chart 15.2. Average Credits Earned by High School Students by Type of Course Work: 1982–2000.

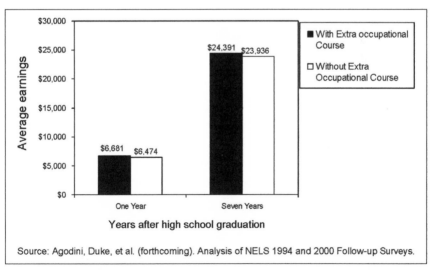

Source: Agodini, Duke, et al. (forthcoming). Analysis of NELS 1994 and 2000 Follow-up Surveys.

Chart 15.3. Post-High School Income Earnings with and without High School Vocational Classes.

- Secondary vocational education has not been a widely effective strategy for improving academic achievement or transition to college.
- Vocational teachers were less likely to have the academic preparation that academic core teachers had obtained, and they perceived that they did not have sufficient professional development on the "key strategies" for the integration of academic content into their various course offerings.
- Vocational teachers scored lower on basic reading and writing tests (PRAXIS) than regular elementary and secondary teachers.

Kaufman, Bradby, and Teitelbaum (2000) demonstrated that students who spend more time planning and discussing their vocational plans with teachers and counselors demonstrated higher academic performance. Another study (Gollub et al., 2002) found that students were more motivated to learn and would persist even in the face of difficulty if they found school personally interesting and meaningful and something they valued.

Maxwell and Rubin (2000) studied cohorts of students in a large urban school district and reported that career academy students dropped out less than half the rate for of nonacademy students. Plank (2001) analyzed the National Education Longitudinal Study of 1988, which involved 11,352 students, and reported that the risk of dropping out was highest when students took no CTE courses. In addition, the "at-risk" high school student who did not take one CTE course was reported to be about four times as likely to drop out as a high-risk student with a 3:4 CTE/academic course-taking ratio. The research concluded that there appeared to be solid statistical evidence that CTE course enrollment does play a role in reducing dropout and that this was especially true for the at-risk students. The report purported that when CTE students were involved in coursework with emphasis on learning in both the academic and CTE courses, the dropout rate was positively impacted.

Schools districts that value the vocational and technical development of their students will provide them with research-based programs and extensive opportunities. Geared to student needs and future employability, career and technical programs have much to offer the student, school, and community. The research strongly supports the connection of real-life experiences to the "theoretical" aspects of learning, as well as the need for these programs. In most districts, these programs provide much data proving the necessity of their curricular offerings, the benefits, and the projected needs. The high school curriculum has always viewed the need to supply data as a means for continued existence. In a culture that predominantly views college-bound students with pride and career education students with tolerance, the reality of a near future will challenge these views.

REFLECTIVE QUESTIONS THAT SUPPORT CONTINUOUS IMPROVEMENT

1. What data do we have that indicates our career and technical programs are making a difference in job placements?
2. What follow-up data (post-graduation employment/employer surveys) are presented?
3. What do graduates (one, three, and five years from graduation) recommend regarding programs, courses, and the development of career plans?
4. What types of assessments are used and how are they tied to the curriculum?
5. What level of input do the community and business world have in keeping the curriculum current and viable?
6. What voice do students have in the curricular offerings?
7. What types of student assessments are being utilized? How are these data being used by students, parents, and faculty?
8. How does student learning manifest itself—projects, employment, and further education?
9. What types of career-awareness and career-development programs exist? Are they embedded into the curricula or are they a stand-alone aspect of the curricula? If embedded, how is the opportunity to develop a future sense of self—as a worker—monitored?
10. What types of career-shadowing experiences are offered high school students?
11. What types of career-interest inventories are made available to all students? Are they online or on paper?

DATA SETS THAT COULD BE REPORTED

1. _____ Number of students enrolled in career and technical courses?
2. _____ Number of students who completed a sequence of study in a particular field (such as health science, technology, etc.)?
3. _____ Academic achievement results (results on norm reference-standardized and criterion-referenced tests)?
4. _____ High school completion rates?
5. _____ Enrollment in postsecondary education programs?
6. _____ Internships scheduled and internships completed?
7. _____ Number of certified (in teaching area) teachers in the career and technical programs?
8. _____ Number of collaboration meetings between core academic teachers and career and technical teachers?
9. _____ Number of special-education students enrolled in career and technical classes?
10. _____ Number of minority students enrolled in career and technical classes?
11. _____ Number of low-income students enrolled in career and technical classes?
12. _____ Number of designed student career plans?
13. _____ Number of executed student career plans?
14. _____ Number of career guidance sessions held with individual students?
15. _____ Number of career guidance sessions held with groups of students?
16. _____ Number of career guidance sessions held with/for parents?
17. _____ Number of students who are credentialed in various career and technical fields (such as Cisco and Microsoft certification)?

PROGRAM EVALUATION

18. Program evaluation via surveys, interviews of students, parents, teachers, administrators, and employers?

19. Student evaluations of courses taught in the career and technical education courses?
20. Exit interviews with students?
21. Reports on trend data and assessments?
22. Employment surveys and satisfaction surveys completed by students and employer?

SUMMARY

Is the only path to success one that starts with college prep courses? Current knowledge suggests that in the future, only 25 to 30 percent of the jobs will require a four-year college degree. In order for this country to remain a world power, the mission for education needs to focus on preparing students to become active participants in our democracy. Additionally, our graduates need to have the knowledge and skills to succeed in a global information economy. This means preparing students at the high school and postsecondary level with the career and technical skills to become employed and economically self-sufficient.

What is fundamentally clear is the need for a paradigm shift from the beliefs that success in life requires a college education. Secondary educators, counselors, administrators, and parents need to reevaluate their beliefs about college prep versus career and technical preparation. It seems that there is bias against having a goal of immediate employment after high school, or that students planning for community college are somehow "less than" when compared to a four-year college students. This fundamental bias limits access, resources, and opportunities, not only for individuals but for our nation.

RESOURCES FOR ADDITIONAL INFORMATION

The Association for Career and Technical Education (ACTE). http://www.acteonline.org/about/index.cfm

Office of Vocational and Adult Education. http://www.ed.gov/about/offices/list/ovae/pi/cte/index.html

Vocational Information Center: Career Exploration. http://www.khake.com/page2.html

Carl Perkins Act—http://www.ade.state.az.us/cte/downloads/PerkinsIV081206.pdf

16

TECHNOLOGY—
"THE FUTURE IS NOW"

Basically my point is this: technology can only go so far to teach students. A massive reform is needed to give staff members a wake up call; the people who are only in for the free ride are the ones who hurt the students' education. More passionate teachers are needed, because these are the ones who will inspire students in their education.

Steve Jobs, March 2007, Apple Matters

Are we preparing students for our past or their future?

Willard Daggett

ESSENTIAL QUESTIONS

What is the technological gap between what is in place and what must be in place to compete in global economy?

What impact should be expected from the investment of technology in the schools?

DEFINITIONS

Technology—Generally associated with computer hardware and other electronic equipment that makes life easier, but realistically technology could be something as simple as an ordinary pencil.

Instructional Technology/Educational Technology—Using multimedia technologies or audiovisual aids as a tool to enhance the teaching and learning process (see International Technology Education Association, http://www.iteawww.org/).

Technology Integration—the seamless utilization of hardware and software into instruction and learning.

Twenty-first Century—a time term that reflects *today*, not some point "out there in the future." For many, the twenty-first century is less about real time and more of a representation of an immediate need to change.

Industrial Age—the economical, philosophical, and political period of American history where factories, mass-production, and prosperity dominated. Many of us understand that we are no longer living in the Industrial Age (evidenced by our cell phones, increased service industry, and closed factories), but we have had difficulty wrapping our minds around what a "knowledge economy" requires of us.

Knowledge Economy—Taken from the title of chapter 12 of Peter Drucker's book, *The Age of Discontinuity*, it has developed into the following definition: A knowledge economy focuses on the production of knowledge and the management of information.

We cannot talk about educational technology without framing it in a glimpse into "today." It is difficult, if not impossible, to keep up with all of the changes and/or improvements as a result of the advancement of technology. Not long ago, computers filled a large room in order to do simple binary functions; however today, they can manage your home, your money, and your life while fitting into the palm of your hand.

Unlike previous chapters, this issue of technology here has multiple layers of complexity. These layers are comprised of pieces of emotional, psychological, historical, and financial layers, each interwoven into the others, complicating an already complex picture. For example, we have children born into this new millennium who have known nothing but instant contact with everyone they want, whether by cell phone, internet, instant messaging, or text messaging. These same children are being taught by teachers who remember when phone lines required discretion when speaking over the wires.

Data are reported that as of 2004 our nation had invested 66 billion dollars in public school technology (Quality Education Data [QED], 2004). It is not unreasonable to ask what the taxpayers received for their fiscal investment. During the 1980s and early 1990s, states put millions of dollars into the hands of schools and districts, often requiring that the purchase of hardware and software be tied to required training (QED, 2004). For example, *Meeting the Challenge* grants in Illinois were one such opportunity. Districts were mandated to spend a minimum of 25 percent of the grant dollars on teacher training. When your students are entry-level with technology, progress toward integration will be slow. Add to that the fact that there were no existing instructional models, and it is not surprising that the training and equipment had little impact on student learning. Couple this reality with the inadequate infrastructures that existed (and still exist) in our nineteenth- and twentieth-century buildings. In too many schools, when more than four or five devices are plugged into the circuit, circuits blow. Although money is only a part of the solution, it is inappropriate practice to train teachers on equipment that they have to share or don't have easy access to. Equipment becomes outdated before it is even delivered, and software updates can bankrupt a district.

As districts look for the "silver bullet" for improving test scores, technology has become a common solution. Districts are purchasing expensive software and hardware packages with too little research-basis for their decisions. Districts need to be clear about the expected outcomes before purchases are made. Professional development and the expectations of the complete utilization of any program should not be optional but instead tied into the teacher evaluation and performance process. District leadership also has the responsibility for presenting a thoughtful, collaboratively designed implementation plan. Districts have the obligation of purchasing all of the needed components (sufficient server, computers, copies or licenses, trainers) to support the successful implementation of a program. Clearly aligning standards, high district expectations, local assessments, and targeted student's characteristics and needs must be the framework for program implementation. Additionally, districts must require a strong program-evaluation process in place prior to expenditures. What will be the impact of this program on student learning and achievement?

RESEARCH

Despite the billions of dollars spent since the Apple IIe found its way into classrooms, little independent empirical research has been conducted connecting technology to improved student performance. There is no shortage of research sponsored by software and hardware companies, but one must be cautious when these results are published. Additionally, the areas of potential research grow exponentially with each new piece of hardware and/or software, while research in other areas becomes obsolete. For example, the research on distance learning ten years ago focused on satellite-linked courses; today it focuses on courses offered over the Internet. Different delivery systems require in some cases different research agendas and questions. This rapid turnover of research questions is part of the reason for the shortage.

A dilemma exists for schools and communities—while "waiting" for funding to purchase equipment and software, to update buildings/classrooms, and to convince teachers that teaching needs to be different, twenty-four states have started online schools. Students participate for various reasons: a desire for a course that their school doesn't offer, for AP classes, for better schedules and/or jobs (Mehta, 2007).

> In the average public school, 3.8 students share every computer used for instructional purposes, Market Data Retrieval (MDR) data show. In some states, such as Maine and South Dakota, schools have an average of only two students for each computer. At the other extreme, the student-to-computer ratio exceeds the 5-to-1 mark in California, New Hampshire, and Utah, a level of computer access less than half of that found in the leading states. (Swanson, 2006, p. 52)

Only about twenty states have stepped in to provide effective and timely leadership by offering interactive databases. Twenty-eight states and the District of Columbia provide access through such a system to current state-assessment results, but five of those states do not include information about how students scored on specific subscale areas or test items (QED,

2004). The federal government has not supplied the means by which schools can compare their test scores with comparable districts/schools.

Dynarski et al. (2007) evaluated math and reading software packages. Effects of the first- and fourth-grade reading and sixth-grade algebra software products were reported as:

a. Ninety-four to 98 percent of the teachers were trained on the products and used them. In the first-grade study, products comprised about 11 percent of the total reading instruction time. In the fourth-grade reading, results indicated that teachers using the software spent about one hour more on reading instruction (8.4 hours a week compared to 7.4 hours for control teachers);
b. effects on test scores for all four studies were not statistically significant; and
c. the fourth-grade reading classroom and school characteristics were correlated with product effects but not so in the other three studies. This difference was found to be statistically significant. Overall differences in test scores were not significantly different, even with the additional time teachers spent on reading.

Schacter (1999) completed a meta-analysis of 700 individual research studies. He concluded that:

students with access to: a) computer assisted instruction or, b) integrated learning systems technology, or c) simulations and software that teaches higher order thinking, or d) collaborative networked technologies or, e) design and programming technologies showed positive gains in achievement on researcher constructed tests, standardized tests, and national tests. (p. 9)

WHERE TO BEGIN?

It is vital that the district have a well-developed technology plan that is aligned to the District Improvement Plan. Discussions should not just focus on the technology but also upon the desired student outcomes. An effective question stem would be, "What is it that you want your students to know and be able to do (for example in first grade or AP Calculus)?" Once you have determined what fundamental knowledge and skills you desire, then you can begin to plan and organize the technology to assist in the accomplishment of those outcomes. For example, a common desire for most communities is the development of children who are effective problem-solvers. Couple that goal with what research states about effective instruction and the district might install and then train its teachers in software packages that deal with real-world problems. At this point, a determination can be made about how much and what types of hardware would be needed. Many dollars have been spent on equipment and software packages that sat off to the side because of poor planning, poor follow-through, and neglible follow-up.

Levinson and Surratt (2003) noted the superintendent must:

> Choose the right problem and set a measurable goal. The important thing is to pick a large problem not being effectively addressed and to develop a means of addressing it. Most school systems buy technology rather than solutions to problems. By focusing on a problem and identifying an effective solution, there is a significant chance technology will be employed correctly. An example of this would be identifying low-achievement, a year behind grade level as a problem that would encourage staff to seek a curriculum planning, delivery and assessment system as a solution. (para. 8)

Someone once said that the faster the world changes, the more inclined we are to nostalgia, or to want some things to remain unchanged. Do schools fall into that category? Do we project a need for a sense of comfort when we walk into our child's classroom? Do your communities rise up in anger or stand up in praise when the school is doing things differently? The answer to these questions will help define whether your community, state, or nation is truly ready for the competitive global economy that the media keeps talking about, because *different needs to happen* and technology is a part of that difference.

QUESTIONS THAT SUPPORT REFLECTION AND DISCUSSION

1. What data do we have that the expenditures for technology (hardware and software) are making a difference in academic achievement for our PK-12 students?

2. What curricular assessments exist? How are these data reported to students, teachers, administrators, the board, and the community?
3. What is the technological skill level of the teachers and administrators? "Do as I say and not as I do" does not work with today's learners.
4. Does your district have a district technology plan? If so, how often is your technology plan reviewed? Why or why not? Can you effectively plan without one? What function does the technology plan have in the day-to-day operations of the district and within the curriculum?
5. What is the selection and decision-making process for all hardware and software purchases?
6. What is the process of communicating the purchases and the implementation of software packages?
7. Is the technology being utilized in research-based methodologies or is it simply "drill and kill?"
8. Is technology integrated into instruction, creating lessons that highly engage the learner?

DATA SETS THAT COULD BE REPORTED

1. What is the update and review process of the technology plan?
2. What percentage of teachers and administrators are proficient with existing hardware and software? (Data is reported from assessments given to staff. There may not be a need to know the identities of the faculty as much as having reportable data around technology skills.)
3. How many teachers integrate technology into their daily lessons (data obtained via principal walk-throughs)?
4. How much time do students spend on computers per day (reported by grade levels and if needed by teacher)?

SUMMARY

There is little doubt that schools need to push the fast-forward button on change. We need to begin following the gambits we so easily give out to our students: "You need to be flexible." "You need to be a lifelong learner." "A smart kid sets goals for continuous improvement." "Learning is constant and smart people are constantly learning." "Change is a way of life. Look at how much has changed in your lifetime." Yet our students see little evidence of this in their classrooms, which, in many cases, hasn't changed since their grandparents attended school. Even with computers and other technology within the classroom, structures remain the same—"stand and deliver," "test and move onto the next chapter," "math is separate from science, which is separate from literacy."

Today, only 28 percent of twelfth-grade high school students believe that schoolwork is meaningful; 21 percent believe that their courses are interesting; and a mere 39 percent believe that schoolwork will have any bearing on their success in later life (Jukes, 2004, p. 4). If these are the opinions of students who stayed to graduate, one wonders what the opinions might be of those who prematurely exited the system.

Additionally, communities and governments must acknowledge that funding is needed to purchase and maintain state-of-the-art hardware and software packages. It is not, however, recommended that districts receive funding without expectations for deliverance. In the 1980s and 1990s, teachers received equipment and many did not use it. Districts that receive additional funding must commit to implementation frameworks, and consequences must be leveraged when those commitments are not met. Teachers should be expected to use the training and equipment; administrators should be expected to provide quality training to teachers and staff while modeling and monitoring usage; and communities should recognize that preparation for the twenty-first century is more costly than ever before. We see everyday that our workplaces spend millions of dollars upgrading to improve efficiency and productivity, yet governmentally and locally there is continual resistance to fund education at levels that would support newer technology and infrastructures. We can't demand a twenty-first-century education from a nineteenth-century system—it gets tweaked at best.

RESOURCES FOR CONTINUED EXPLORATION

The State Educational Technology Directors Association (SETDA) has released a free online guide designed to help schools achieve more efficient integration of technology. *Profiling Educational Technology Integration (PETI)* (http://www.metiri.com/SETDA/PETI).

International Society for Technology in the Classroom (NETS)—Technology standards for students, teachers, and administrators (http://www.iste.org/).

3D Data-driven Decision-Making. http://www.3d2know.org/

Microsoft Digital Literacy. Five online courses and assessments for knowledge on technology and Microsoft products. Service is free and will print out a certificate showing competency (knowledge) in a number of software applications (http://www.microsoft.com/About/CorporateCitizenship/Citizenship/giving/programs/UP/digitalliteracy/eng/Curriculum.mspx)

Edutopia. A free, online source for innovation and inspiration for K-12 schools. Teacher training, information, research, and much more. George Lucas Foundation supports this website (http://www.edutopia.org/).

eSchool news. A free, online (hard copy also available) source for current research, products, and information related to educational technology (http://www.eschoolnews.com/).

CAUTION: CHANGES AHEAD—WHERE TO FROM HERE?

The most important attitude that can be formed is that of the desire to go on learning.

John Dewey

Caution: The use of data and research must be coupled with an awareness of your community and your students.

Accountability is about sharing responsibility to collectively remove barriers that impede learning and involves *all of the critical players* in a school setting. Accountability is the result of intentional efforts to close the achievement gap and meet the goals of school improvement. (Dahir & Stone, 2003, p. 214)

Current literature informs us that schools and districts are now collecting academic achievement data, thanks to NCLB (2001), but they fall short on analyzing the data and translating the data into strategies that will improve student achievement. The simple collection and reporting of data will not result in continuous improvement. The system must develop diagnostic skills whereby conclusions and recommendations are based upon a triangulation of data points.

There is *hope*, however. In 1983, a landmark federal report was released that forecasted major national concerns regarding the potential
loss of American positioning in the global marketplace. As a result of this
report, our nation stepped up and the forecasted outcomes did not find
their place in our reality. It is unfortunate, however to read the report
and realize how little has changed since it was published. The same
problems continue to plague our nation. We believe it would be worth-
while to quote the first five paragraphs of *A Nation at Risk* (National
Commission on Excellence in Education, 1983).

All, regardless of race or class or economic status, are entitled to a fair
chance and to the tools for developing their individual powers of mind
and spirit to the utmost. This promise means that all children by virtue of their own efforts, competently guided, can hope to attain the
mature and informed judgment needed to secure gainful employment,
and to manage their own lives, thereby serving not only their own interests but also the progress of society itself.

Our Nation is at risk. Our once unchallenged preeminence in commerce, industry, science, and technological innovation is being overtaken
by competitors throughout the world. This report is concerned with only
one of the many causes and dimensions of the problem, but it is the one
that undergirds American prosperity, security, and civility. We report to
the American people that while we can take justifiable pride in what our
schools and colleges have historically accomplished and contributed to the
United States and the well-being of its people, the educational foundations of our society are presently being eroded by a rising tide of medi-
ocrity that threatens our very future as a Nation and a people. What was
unimaginable a generation ago has begun to occur—others are matching
and surpassing our educational attainments.

If an unfriendly foreign power had attempted to impose on America
the mediocre educational performance that exists today, we might well
have viewed it as an act of war. As it stands, we have allowed this to
happen to ourselves. We have even squandered the gains in student
achievement made in the wake of the Sputnik challenge. Moreover, we
have dismantled essential support systems which helped make those gains
possible. We have, in effect, been committing an act of unthinking, unilat-
eral educational disarmament.

Our society and its educational institutions seem to have lost sight of
the basic purposes of schooling, and of the high expectations and disci-

plined effort needed to attain them. This report, the result of 18 months of study, seeks to generate reform of our educational system in fundamental ways and to renew the Nation's commitment to schools and colleges of high quality throughout the length and breadth of our land.

That we have compromised this commitment is, upon reflection, hardly surprising, given the multitude of often conflicting demands we have placed on our Nation's schools and colleges. They are routinely called on to provide solutions to personal, social, and political problems that the home and other institutions either will not or cannot resolve. We must understand that these demands on our schools and colleges often exact an educational cost as well as a financial one. (p. 6)

In many respects, these words could have been written yesterday, not twenty-four years ago. Yet the forecasts proved to be wrong, as our nation rose to the occasion and remained a great nation. Just as we tell our students and our children, we cannot predict tomorrow based upon yesterday, for they are too different in their substances—there are too many variables that are too different. What we do know is that we are up to this similar yet new global challenge—we have the capability and we have no choice.

ESSENTIAL QUESTIONS

1. Whose responsibility is it to establish a vision for public school education for the United States of America?
2. What level of responsibility must be assumed by state officials in determining "what is best" for children in their states?
3. How can a system be created that examines and utilizes scientific-based research and data for short- *and* long-term planning? Budgets and calendars are only established for one year at a time—is this the best practice? Legislation is not a plan!
4. How does the public develop for all PK-12 children an integrated service and educational delivery system that builds bridges of communication, shares impact, and focuses on results (not on territories or scarcity of funds)?
5. How will public education in this country bridge the gap between what is comfortable and known in terms of structure and

function and what needs to be happening for the twenty-first-century learner?

6. How can we more effectively utilize existing education dollars for the intellectual and socio-emotional advancement of every child?

7. What types of data and evidence need to be supplied to the public supporting the continuation of existing programs?

8. What needs to happen for local control to effectively improve the education of *all* learners within every community?

9. What fiscal and programmatic accountability systems exist and are used within each school district?

10. What needs to happen within a community for the stakeholders to take ownership for *all* children within their community?

11. How do you move a dysfunctional school/district culture into an exemplary culture of achievement?

12. How do you keep individuals/groups passionate about "doing the right thing for kids"—not the contract, not the adults, not the schedule, but kids? How do you keep them motivated and in the field of education?

13. How do you view the twenty-first-century work-force needs and the constantly changing world around us and continue to support a traditional curriculum, traditional schedules, traditional report cards, and traditional teaching (is there one right answer)?

ADDITIONAL QUESTIONS FOR REFLECTION AND DIALOGUE

These questions have surfaced since we began this project. As you can see, the depth of using data to drive decision-making is bottomless.

1. What relationship exists between the data being reported to you and the district mission, vision, and goals?

2. How are school-improvement days being used? What evidence do you have of their impact upon student learning and achievement?

3. What data are you receiving on school culture/climate? On school board climate/culture?

4. What system do you have in place to recognize exemplary students and teachers?

5. How do you know teacher evaluations have been used effectively?

6. How many personnel have been released or reassigned?

7. What is the role of the central office in student achievement? What data do you have that the central office personnel are serving the schools?

8. What data are you receiving about the recruitment and retention of highly qualified teachers?

9. What does your data on teacher attendance tell you?

10. How are parent-involvement activities/programs being evaluated (work smarter, not harder)?

11. What do you do regarding succession planning?

12. What district data (strategic planning, external audits, etc.) have been collected in the past three years *and* how were they used?

13. If you had to go before a judge and provide evidence that the most highly qualified individuals fill your administrative positions, would you be able to?

14. What data do you have regarding special education and its effectiveness? How many students are referred? How many serviced? How many get in and never get out? How many IEP goals are the same year after year? How well written are the IEPs?

15. How effective are your title programs?

16. How effective are your school lawyers? (In one school district, a teacher was determined to have stolen $20,000. The school lawyer advised the superintendent to let the teacher pay it back and hope that it didn't become a "big deal." What type of advice was that? What consequences do you think a student in that district would receive for stealing $100 from a teacher's desk? What type of system supports double standards?

17. How is data triangulated?

18. How are speech and language therapists being used? What data do we have giving evidence of their impact?

HOW TO DEVELOP AN EVALUATION PLAN

1. *Caution*: In many cases, there is less of a need to generate new data than there is to effectively utilize what is already present. Does the data that you need already exist? If so, how is it being used and reported?

2. *Caution*: More is not better. Overwhelming everyone with a need for data can actually drain the resource of time away from the "good work" that is going on within a department, grade level, or division. Brainstorm with your stakeholders to determine what the essential questions are for your district/building and then get the data needed to answer the question(s). Request that the data effectively be reported by all: gender, ethnicity, income level, and program level(s) (such as students in Title I, extended learning, special education, counseling and other student support services, gifted, etc.). For example, if it looks like you have a dropout problem, find out exactly who these students are. Are they low-income, female, and gifted? How can you determine a "treatment plan" without specifically identifying the "patient?" Examining aggregate groups, for example, all dropouts, and not digging deeper leaves us with "treating" everyone the same—and of course, we know they are not the same.

3. *Caution:* Don't spend all of your time looking at numbers and not enough time viewing success. Celebrate *all* that is going right within your classrooms, schools, buildings, and district, and do so with frequency!

4. Understand that if your district or school does not have a program-evaluation system in place, asking your staff and/or administrators to plan one overnight may result in negative outcomes. Realize that change takes at least three years, and often up to five, before a systematic process of collecting the data, disaggregating the data, and using the data to drive continuous improvement happens. It is wise leadership that establishes a big picture of all of the pieces of data and the different programs (Title-I and all other Title programs, special-education, grade-level data, building reports, gifted, vocational education, department, evaluations/personnel, etc.) and determines a rotating

schedule of reporting. A communication plan for sharing reports and results could also be created. Examples of methods of reporting might include: posting the report/results to the district/school Web pages; posting in simple brochures; and distributing through news releases, public meetings, programs, etc.

It is our belief that a teacher is an ultimate environmentalist: preserving, protecting, and nurturing our greatest natural resource. As John Kennedy once said:

"Our progress as a nation can be no swifter than our progress in education. . . . The human mind is our most fundamental resource."

John and Pat Samara
The Curriculum Project

REFERENCES

Action for Healthy Kids (2002). *Taking action for healthy kids: A report on the healthy schools summit and the action for healthy kids initiative.* Retrieved January 3, 2007, from http://www.actionforhealthykids.org/

Allen, R. (2002, November). Teachers and paraeducators: Defining roles in an age of accountability. *Educational Update*, 44(7), 1–2, Association of Supervision and Curriculum Development.

Alston, F. K. (2007). Latch key children. NYU Child Study Center. Retrieved March 2, 2007, from http://www.aboutourkids.org/research/studies.html

American Association of Colleges for Teacher Educations (2001, March). *PK-12 educational leadership and administration. A white paper.* Washington, DC: American Association of Colleges for Teacher Education.

American Association of School Administrators (n.d.). *Using data to improve schools: What's working.* Report funded by the Office of Educational Research and Improvement, Washington, DC. American Association of School Administrators.

American Association of State Colleges and Universities (2005). The facts and fictions about teacher shortages. *Policy Matters*, 2(5), 1–4.

American Federation of Teachers: Paraprofessionals and School-Related Personnel (2006, November 19). *Survey of paraprofessionals on assignments post-NCLB.* Retrieved November 26, 2007, from http://www.aft.org/psrp/topics/download/NCLB2006ParaSurvey.pdf

American Lung Association (2006, August). *Asthma & children fact sheet.* Retrieved March 22, 2007, from http://www.lungusa.org/site/pp.asp?c=dvLUK9OOE&b=44352

Americans for the Arts (2005). *What can school board leaders do?* Retrieved March 11, 2007, from http://ww3.americansforthearts.org/services/arts_education/resource_center/resource_center_008.asp#

Ashbaker, B. Y., & Morgan, J. (2000–2001). Paraeducators: A powerful human resource.

Streamlined Seminar, 19(1), 1–3. ERIC Document Reproduction Service No. ED453573.

Bell, E. (2001, September 23). *Schools' principal shortage: Fewer teachers want the job's growing challenges*. San Francisco Chronicle. (On-line at http://sfgate.com /cgi-bin/article.cgi?file=/chronicle/archive/2001/09/23/MN170314.DTL).

Black, S. (2006). Head of the class: Through distributed leadership, the superintendent can play a vital role in raising student achievement. *American School Board Journal, 193*(2), 32–36, National Boards Association.

Blasé, J., & Blasé, J. (1999). Principals' instructional leadership and teacher development: Teachers' perspectives. *Educational Administration Quarterly, 35*(3), 349–380.

Borders, L. D., & Drury, S. M. (1992, March/April). Comprehensive school counseling programs: A review for policymakers and practitioners. *Journal of Counseling and Development, 70*, 487–498.

Buchanan, B. (2004). *Turnover at the top*. American School Boards Journal Special Report. Retrieved May 21, 2001, from http://www.asbj.com/specialreports /2004SpecialReports/S1.html

Burton, J., Horowitz, R., & Abeles, H. (2000, Spring). Learning in and through the arts: The question of transfer. *Studies in Art Education, 41*(3), 228–257.

Canton, J. (2006). *The extreme future: The top trends that will reshape the world for the next 5, 10, and 20 years*. New York: Dutton Adult.

Carl D. Perkins Career & Technical Improvement Act of 2006. Retrieved March 1, 2007, from http://www.ed.gov.policy (Pub.L.No. 109–270).

Carns, A. W., & Carns, M. R. (1991). Teaching study skills, cognitive strategies, and metacognitive skills through self-diagnosed learning styles. *The School Counselor, 38*, 341–346.

Carlson, N. N. (2004). *School counselors' knowledge, perceptions, and involvement concerning gifted and talented students*. (Doctoral dissertation, University of Maryland College Park).

Catterall, J. S. (2002, September). Book summary: Critical links: Learning in the arts and student social and academic development. *New Horizons for Learning*. Retrieved February 23, 2005, from http://www.newhorizons.org/strategies/arts/catterall.htm

Catterall, J. S. (1998). Involvement in the arts and success in secondary school. *American for the Arts Monographs, 1*(9), 4–16.

Catterall, J. S., Chapleau, R., & Iwanaga, J. (2005). *Involvement in the arts and human development: Extending an analysis of general associations and introducing the special cases of intensive involvement in music and theatre arts*. The Imagination Project at UCLA Graduate School of Education & Information Studies University of California at Los Angeles. Retrieved June 28, 2007, from http://www.livemusictaskforce. org/media/arts-and-human-development.pdf

Catterall, J. S., & Waldorf, L. (2002). Chicago Arts Partnership in Education (CAPE): Evaluation summary. In R. Deasy (Ed.), *Critical links: Learning in the arts and student achievement and social development*. Washington, DC: Arts Education Program.

Centers for Disease Control and Prevention (2004). *Summary health statistics for U.S. children: National heath interview survey, 2002*. Series 10(221). U.S. Department of Health and Human Services, Washington, DC: U.S. Government Printing Office.

Chapman, L. H. (2004). No child left behind in art? *Arts Education Policy Review, 106*(2), 3–17.

Christian, D. (1996). Two-way immersion education: Students learning through two languages. *Modern Language Journal, 80*(1), 66–76.

Clark, F. L. (2002). Zero-tolerance discipline: The effect of teacher discretionary removal on urban minority students. Dissertation University of Texas at Austin. Retrieved March 22, 2007, from http://dspace.lib.utexas.edu/bitstream/2152/1158/1/clarkfl026.pdf

Cohen, A. D. (1975). *A sociolinguistic approach to bilingual education.* Rowley, MA: Newbury House.

Colangeloc, N., Assouline, S. G., & Gross, M. U. M. (2004a). *A nation deceived: How schools hold back America's brightest students. Volume 1.* The Templeton National Report on Acceleration. Retrieved June 28, 2007, from http://www.education.uiowa.edu/belinblank

Colangelo, N., Assouline, S. G., & Gross, M. U. M. (2004b). *A nation deceived: How schools hold back America's brightest students. Volume 2.* The Templeton National Report on Acceleration. Retrieved June 28, 2007, from http://www.education.uiowa.edu/belinblank

Colangelo, N., & Davis, G. A. (Eds.) (2003). *The handbook of gifted education.* Boston: Pearson Education.

Colgan, C. (2005). The new look of school safety. *American School Board Journal, 192*(3), 10–13.

College Board SAT. (2006). *2006 college-bound seniors: Total group profile report.* Retrieved March 12, 2007, from http://www.collegeboard.com/prod_downloads/about/news_info/cbsenior/yr2006/national-report.pdf

Cooper, H., Charlton, K., Valentine, J., & Muhlenbruck, L. (2000) *Making the most of summer school.* Malden, MA: Blackwell.

Cortez, A. (2003). The emerging majority: The growth of the Latino population and Latino student enrollments. Retrieved August 25, 2006, from http://www.idra.org/IDRA_Newsletters/January_2003:_Self_Renewing_Schools

Cotton, K. (2003). *Principals and student achievement: What the research says.* Alexandria, VA: Association of Supervision and Curriculum Development.

Covey, S. R. (2004). *The eighth habit.* New York: Simon & Schuster—Free Press.

Cryan, J., et al. (1992). Success outcomes of full-day kindergarten: More positive behavior and increased achievement in the years after. *Early Childhood Research Quarterly, 7*(2), 187–203.

Csikszentmihalyi, M. (1997). Assessing aesthetic education. *Grantmakers in the Arts, 8*(1), 22–26.

Cummins, J. (1991). Interdependence of first- and second-language proficiency in bilingual children. In E. Bialystock (Ed.), *Language processing in bilingual children* (pp. 70–89). Cambridge, UK: Cambridge University Press.

Dahir, C. A., & Stone, C. B. (2003). Accountability: A M.E.A.S.U.R.E of the impact school counselors have on student achievement. *Professional School Counseling, 6*(3), 214–221. American School Counselors Association.

Dame, M. H. (1994). Supporting student achievement skills. *Language, Speech, and Hearing Services in Schools, 25*, pp. 34–36.

Darling-Hammond, L. (1998). Teacher learning that supports student learning. *Educational Leadership, 55*(5), 6–11.

Darling-Hammond, L., & McLaughlin, M. W. (1996). Policies that support professional development in an era of reform. In M.W. McLaughlin and I. Oberman (Eds.),

Teacher Learning: New Policies, New Practices (pp. 202–218). New York: Teachers College Press, Columbia University.

Darling-Hammond, L., & McLaughlin, M. W. (1995). *Teacher learning that supports student learning.* New York: The National Commission on Teaching and America's Future. Retrieved August 21, 2006, from http://www.edutopia.org/php/article .php?id=Art_478&key=238

Deasy, R. J. (Ed.). (2002a). *Champions of change: The impact of the arts on learning.* Washington, DC: Arts Education Partnership. Retrieved March 12, 2007, from http://www.livemusictaskforce.org/media/arts-and-human-development.pdf

Deasy, R. J. (Ed.). (2002b). *Critical links: Learning in the arts and student achievement and social development.* Washington, DC: Arts Education Partnership. Retrieved March 12, 2007, from http://www.aep-arts.org/resources/toolkits/criticallinks /criticallinks.pdf

Department of Health and Human Services, CDC. (2006, January 13). Overweight among students in grades K-12. Arkansas, 2003–04 and 2004–05 School Years. *Morbidity and Mortality Weekly Report, 55*(01), 5–8. Atlanta, GA: Centers for Disease Control and Prevention. Retrieved August 27, 2006, from http://www.cdc.gov/mmwr /preview/mmwrhtml/mm5501a2.htm

Dibble, N. (1999). *Outcome evaluation of school social work services.* Retrieved March 1, 2007, from http://dpi.state.wi.us/sspw/pdf/outcmeval999.pdf

Dinkes, R., Cataldi, E. F., Kena, G., Baum, K., & Snyder, T. D. (2006, December). *Indicators of school crime and safety: 2006.* National Center for Educational Statistics, Bureau of Justice Statistics, U.S. Department of Education and U.S. Department of Justice. Washington, DC: National Center for Educational Statistics.

Downing, J. E., Ryndak, D. L., & Clark, D. (2000, May/June). Paraeducators in inclusive classrooms: Their own perceptions. *Remedial and Special Educator, 21*(3), 171–181.

Doyle, M. B. (2002). *The paraprofessional's guide to the inclusive classroom: Working as a team.* Baltimore, MD: Brookes.

Druckers, P. (1971). *What we can learn from Japanese management.* Executive Development Series, Part III. Cambridge, MA: Harvard College.

Druckers, P. (1959). *The landmarks of tomorrow.* Somerset, NJ: Transaction Publishers.

DuFour, R. (2004, May). Schools as learning communities. *Educational Leadership, 61*(8), 6–11. Association of Supervision & Curriculum Council.

DuFour, R. (2002). The learning-centered principal. *Educational Leadership, 59*(8), 12–15.

Durlak, J. A., & Weissberg, R. P. (2007). *The impact of after-school programs that promote personal and social skills.* Collaborative for Academic, Social, and Emotional Learning (CASEL). Retrieved March 1, 2007, from http://www.casel.org/downloads /ASP-Exec.pdf

Dwyer, K., Osher, D., & Warger, C. (1998, August). *Early warning, timely response: A guide to safe schools.* Washington, DC: U.S. Department of Education.

Dynarski, M., Agodini, R., Heaviside, S., Novak, T., Carey, N., et al. (2007, March). *Effectiveness of reading and mathematics software products: Findings from the first student cohort. Report to Congress.* The National Center for Education Evaluation and Regional Assistance. Washington, DC: U.S. Department of Education Institute of Education Sciences.

Elicker, J., & Mathur, S. (1997). What do they do all day? Comprehensive evaluation of a full-day kindergarten. *Early Childhood Research Quarterly*, *12*(4), 459–480.

Elliot, J., & Zimmerman, A. (2002). *A comparison between career and technical education and other students on a high stakes test.* Paper presented at the meeting of the Western Region Agriculture Education Conference, Seattle, WA.

Elmore, R. (2004). *School Reform from the Inside Out.* Cambridge, MA: Harvard Education Press.

Etnier, J. L., Salazar, W., Landers, D. M., Petruzzello, S. J., Han, M., & Nowell, P. (1997). The influence of physical fitness and exercise upon cognitive functioning: A meta-analysis. *Journal of Sport and Exercise Psychology*, *19*(3), 249–277.

Evansville-Vanderburgh School Corporation. (1988). *A Longitudinal Study of the Consequences of Full-Day Kindergarten through Grade Eight.* Retrieved June 28, 2007, from www.evsc.k12.in.us/evscinfo/kindergarten/stdy1988.html

Fein, R. A., Vossekuil, B., Pollack, W. S., Borum, R., Modzeleski, W., & Reddy, M. (2002, May). *Threat assessment in schools: A guide to managing threatening situations and to creating safe school climates.* U.S. Secret Service and U.S. Department of Education, Washington, DC.

Fielding, L., Kerr, N., & Rosier, P. (2004). *Delivering on the promise of the 95% reading and math.* Kennewick, WA: New Foundation.

Fitzpatrick, K. (1997). *School improvement: Focusing on student performance.* Schaumburg, IL: National Study of School Evaluation.

Flowers, N., Mertens, S. B., & Melhall, P. F. (2002). Four important lessons about teacher professional development. *Middle School Journal*, *33*(5), 57–61.

Friedman, T. L. (2006). *The world is flat: A brief history of the twenty-first century.* New York, NY: Farrar, Straus and Giroux.

French, N. K. (2007). *The paraeducator effectiveness study: Paraeducator training, effectiveness and student achievement.* The PARA center. Retrieved March 1, 2007, from http://www.paracenter.org/AboutUs/CurrentProjects/ResearchProjects/ParaeducatorEffectivenessStudy

Fullan, M. (1979). *School-focused in-service education in Canada.* Report prepared for Centre for Educational Research and Innovation, Paris.

Fullan, M., & Stiegelbauer, S. (1991). *The meaning of educational change.* New York: Teachers College.

Gallagher, J. J., Clifford, R. M., & Maxwell, K. (2004). Getting from here to there: To an ideal early preschool system. *Early Childhood Research & Practice* 6(1). Retrieved October, 2, 2006, from http://ecrp.uiuc.edu/v6n1/clifford.html

Garet, M. S., Porter, A. C., Desimone, L., Birman, B. F., & Yoon, K. S. (2001). What makes professional development effective? Results from a national sample of teachers. *American Educational Research Journal*, *4*, 915–945.

Gates, S., et al. (2003). *Who is leading our schools?* Rand Corporation. Prepared for the Wallace Reader's Digest Funds. Retrieved April 1, 2007, from http://www.rand.org/

Gay, G. (2001). Preparing for culturally responsive teaching. *Journal of Teacher Education*, *53*, 106–115.

Genesee, F. (1987). Considering two-way bilingual programs. *Equity and Choice*, *3*(3), 3–7.

Gerber, S. B., Finn, J. D., Achilles, C. M., & Boyd-Zaharias, J. (2001). Teacher aides and students' academic achievement. *Educational Evaluation and Policy Analysis,*

23(2), 123–143.

Ghere, G., & York-Barr, J. (2003, July). *Employing, developing, and directing special education paraprofessionals in inclusive education programs: Findings of a multi-site case study.* Institute on Community Integration & Department of Educational Policy and Administration, University of Minnesota. Retrieved March 1, 2007, from http://ici.umn.edu/products

Giangreco, M. F. (2003). Working with paraprofessionals. *Educational Leadership*, 61(2), 50–53.

French, N. (1998). *Working together.* Paraprofessional Academy. Denver, CO: University of Colorado at Denver, Center for Collaborative Educational Leadership.

Giangreco, M. F., Broer, S. M., & Edelman, S. W. (2001). Teacher engagement with students with disabilities: Differences between paraprofessional service delivery models. *Journal of the Association for Persons with Severe Handicaps*, 26, 75–86.

Ginsburg, A. L. (1992). *Improving bilingual education programs through evaluation.* Proceedings of the Second National Research Symposium on Limited English Proficient Student Issues: Focus on Evaluation and Measurement. OBEMLA, U.S. Department of Education. Retrieved March 26, 2005, from http://www.ncela.gwu.edu/pubs/symposia/second/vol1/improving.htm#Improving

Gitlin, A., Buendía, E., Crossland, K., & Doumbia, F. (2003). The production of margin and center: Welcoming–unwelcoming of immigrant students. *American Educational Research Journal*, 40, 91–122.

Gladwell, M. (2000). *Tipping point: How little things can make a difference.* Boston, MA: Little, Brown and Company.

Glass, T. E., Bjork, L., & Brunner, C. C. (2000). *The study of the American school superintendency: 2000.* Arlington, VA: American Association of School Administrators.

Gollub, J., Bertenthal, M., Labov, J., & Curtis, P. (2002). *Learning and understanding: Improving advanced study of U.S. high schools.* Washington, DC: National Research Council.

Granger, J. D., & Grek, M. (2005, Summer). Struggling readers stretch their skills: Project maximizes use of paraprofessionals to teach reading. *Journal of Staff Development*, 26(3), 1–4.

Greene, M. (1995). *Releasing the imagination: Essays on education, the arts, and social change.* New York: Teachers College Press.

Greenfield, P. M. (1997). You can't take it with you: Why ability assessments don't cross cultures. *American Psychologist*, 52, 1115–1124.

Gunzelmann, B. (2004, fall). Hidden dangers within our schools: What are these safety problems and how can we fix them? *Educational Horizons*, 83(1), 66–76.

Guskey, T. R. (1994). The most significant advances in the field of staff development over the last twenty-five years. *Journal of Staff Development*, 15(4), 5–6.

Hakuta, K., Butler, Y. G., & Witt, D. (2000). *How long does it take English language learners to attain proficiency? Policy Report 2000–1.* The University of California Linguistic Minority Research Institute, Stanford University.

Hardy, L. (2004). The well-trained aide. *American School Board Journal*, 191(10), 33–34. National School Boards Association.

Harland, J., Kinder, K., Lord, P., Stott, A., Schagen, I., Haynes, J., et al. (2000). Effectiveness of arts education. In *Arts Education in Secondary Schools: Effects and Effectiveness.* Slough: National Foundation Educational Research.

Harper, C., & Platt, E. (1998). Full inclusion for secondary school ESOL students: Some concerns from Florida. *TESOL Journal*, 7(5), 30–36.

Harris, S. L., & Lowery, S. (2002). A view from the classroom. *Educational Leadership*, 59(8), 64–65.

Hart, B., & Risely, T. R. (1995). *Meaningful differences in the everyday experience of young American children*. Baltimore: Paul H. Brookes.

Haycock, K., & Chenoweth, K. (2005, April). Choosing to make a difference: How schools and districts are beating the odds and narrowing the achievement gap. *American School Board Journal*, 191(4), 28–32.

Hedley, A. A., Ogden, C. L., Johnson, C. L., Carroll, M. D., Curtin, L. R., & Flegal, K. M. (2004). Prevalence of overweight and obesity among U.S. children, adolescents, and adults, 1999–2002. *Journal of American Medical Association*, 291, 2847–2850.

Hetland, H. (2000). Learning to make music enhances spatial reasoning. *The Journal of Aesthetic Education*, 34(3–4), 179–238.

Hirsch, S. (1997). Everyone benefits when teachers lead. *School Team Innovator*. Retrieved February 2, 2007, from http://www.nsdc.org/library/publications/innovator/inn3-97hirsh.cfm

Hornbeck, M. (2003). What your district's budget is telling you? *Journal of Staff Development*, 24(3) 2–4.

Hough, D., & Bryde, S. (1996). *The effects of full-day kindergarten on student achievement and affect*. Paper presented at the Annual Conference of the American Educational Research Association, New York, NY. Retrieved January 31, 2007, from ERIC database.

Housden, T., & Kam, R. (1992). *Full-day kindergarten: A summary of the research*. Carmichael, CA: San Juan United School District. Retrieved January 31, 2007, from ERIC database.

Howell, J. C., & Lynch, J. P. (2000, August). Youth gangs in schools. *Juvenile Justice Bulletin*, U.S. Department of Justice: Office of Justice Programs, Washington, DC: Office of Juvenile Justice and Delinquency Preventions.

Howley, A., & Pendarvis, E. (2003). Recruiting and retaining rural school administrators. *Eric Digest*. Retrieved May 7, 2007, from http://www.ericdigest.org/2003-4/rural-administrators.html

Hurley, S. R., & Blake, S. (2000). Assessment in the content areas for students acquiring English. In S. R. Hurley & J. V. Tinajero (Eds.), *Literacy assessment of second language learners* (pp. 84–103). Boston: Allyn and Bacon.

Hvrjscl (2006, August 30). Clark County faces teacher shortage as classes begin. *Las Vegas Sun*. Retrieved May 20, 2007, from http://ww.lasvegassun.com/sunbin/stoires/nevada/2006/aug/30/083010337.html

Hyman, I. A., & Perone, D. C. (1998). The other side of school violence: Educator policies and practices that may contribute to student misbehavior. *Journal of School Psychology*, 36(1), 7–27.

Ingersoll, R. M. (2003, September). *Is there really a teacher shortage?* University of Washington, Center for the Study of Teaching and Policy, National Research Consortium. Retrieved April 23, 2007, from http://depts.washington.edu/ctpmail/PDFs/Turnover-Ing-01-2001.pdf

Ingersoll, R. (2003). *Is there a teacher shortage?* Seattle, WA: Center for the Study of Teaching and Policy.

Ingersoll, R. M. (2001, January). *Teacher turnover, teacher shortages, and the organization of schools.* University of Washington: Center for the Study of Teaching and Policy: A National Research Consortium. Retrieved April 23, 2007, from http://depts .washington.edu/ctpmail/PDFs/Turnover-Ing-01-2001.pdf

Jacob, B. A. (2007). The challenge of staffing urban schools with effective teachers. *The Future of Children, 17*(1). 129–153

Johnson, S., & Johnson, C. D. (2003). Results-based guidance: A systems approach to student support programs. *Professional School Counseling, 6*(3), 180–184. American School Counselor Association.

Johnson, P. B. (2004). The relationship between average SAT scores (total, verbal, and math) and concert festival participation in South Carolina public high schools. (Doctoral dissertation, Georgia Southern University). *Dissertation Abstracts International, 65*(8), 2851A.

Jones, R. C. (2006). *Living with HIV/AIDS: Students tell their stories of stigma, courage, and resilience.* Alexandria, VA: National School Boards Association.

Jones, K. H., & Bender, W. N. (1993). Utilization of paraprofessionals in special education: A review of the literature. *Remedial and Special Education, 14*, 7–14.

Juel, C. (1988). Learning to read and write: A longitudinal study of 54 children from first through fourth grades. *Journal of Educational Psychology, 80*, 437–447.

Juel, C., Griffith, P., & Gough, P. (1986). Acquisition of literacy: A longitudinal study of children in first and second grade. *Journal of Educational Psychology, 78*, 243–255.

Jukes, I. (2004). *Windows on the future: Being infosavvy in the information age.* The InfoSavvy Group. Retrieved on March 1, 2007, from http://skyways.lib.ks.us /tricon/2004/handouts/infosavvy.pdf

Karoly, L. A., Kilburn, M. R., & Cannon, J. S. (2005). *Early childhood interventions: Proven results, future promise.* Santa Monica, CA: Rand Corp.

Karweit, N. (1992). The kindergarten experience. *Educational Leadership, 49*(6), 82–86.

Kaufman, J. (1997, June 2). *Evaluation summary report of full-day kindergarten program.* Wisconsin Department of Public Instruction.

Kaufman, P., Bradby, D., & Teitelbaum, P. (2000). *High schools that work and whole school reform: Academic achievement of vocational completers through reform of school practices.* Berkeley, CA: National Center for Research in Vocational Education, University of California, Berkeley.

Killion, J. (2003). 8 smooth steps: Solid footwork makes evaluating professional development programs a song. *Journal of Staff Development, 24*(4), 14–26.

Killion, J. (2002a). *What works in the high school: Results-based staff development to advance the conversations.* Oxford, OH: National Staff Development Council. Retrieved May 22, 2006, from http://www.nsdc.org/connect/projects/hswhatworks.pdf

Killion, J. (2002b). *Assessing impact: Evaluating staff development.* Oxford, OH: National Staff Development Council. Retrieved March 2, 2007, from http://www.nsdc .org/library/publications/innovator/inn3-97hirsh.cfm

Killion, J. (1999). *Islands of hope in a sea of dreams: A research project on the eight schools that received the national award for model professional development.* Report prepared for U. S. Department of Education and WestEd Regional Laboratory.

Kirk, B. V. (2002). Two-way bilingual immersion: A portrait of quality schooling. *Bilingual Research Journal, 26*(1). Retrieved December 4, 2005, from http://brj.asu .edu/content/vol26_no1/html/art6.htm

Krashen, S. D. (1999). *Condemned without a trial: Bogus arguments against bilingual education.* Portsmouth, NH: Heinemann.

Kulik, J. A. (2003). Grouping and tracking. In N. Colangelo & G. A. Davis (Eds.), *Handbook of gifted education*, 3rd ed. (pp. 268–281). Boston: Allyn & Bacon.

Kulik, J. A. (1992). *An analysis of the research on ability grouping: Historical and contemporary perspectives.* Storrs, CT: National Research Center on the Gifted and Talented, University of Connecticut.

Lambert, L. (1998a). How to build leadership capacity. *Educational Leadership*, 55(7), 17–19. Alexandria, VA: Association of Supervision and Curriculum and Development.

Lambert, L. (1998b). *Building leadership capacity in schools.* Alexandria, VA: Association of Supervision and Curriculum Development.

Lambert, W. E., & Tucker, G. R. (1972). *Bilingual education of children: The St. Lambert experiment.* Rowley, MA: Newbury House Publishers.

Lance, K. C., Rodney, M. J., & Hamilton-Pennell, C. H. (2005). *Powerful libraries make powerful learners: The Illinois study.* Illinois School Library Media Association. Retrieved October 30, 2006, from http://www.alliancelibrarysystem.com/illinoisstudy /The_Study.pdf and http://www.lrs.org/impact.asp

Lapan, R. T., Gysbers, N. C., & Petroski, G. F. (2001, Summer). Helping seventh graders be safe and successful: A statewide study of the impact of comprehensive guidance and counseling programs. *Journal of Counseling and Development*, 79(3), 320–330. American Counseling Association.

Lauer, P. A., Akiba, M. W., Wilkerson, S. B., Apthorp, H. S., Snow, D., & Martin-Glenn, M. (2006, summer). Out-of-school time programs: A meta-analysis of effects of at-risk students. *Review of Educational Research*, 76(2), 275–285, 292, 295, 297–298, 300, 303–313. American Educational Research Association.

Lauer, P. A., Akiba, M. W., Wilkerson, S. B., Apthorp, H. S., Snow, D., & Martin-Glenn, M. (2007). The effectiveness of out-of-school-time strategies in assisting low-achieving students in reading and mathematics: A research synthesis. *McREL.* Retrieved March 2, 2007, from http://www.mcrel.org/topics/products/151/

Learning First Alliance (2001). *Every child learning: Safe and supportive schools.* Baltimore, MD: Association of Supervision and Curriculum Development.

Lenski, S. D., Ehlers-Zavala, F., Daniel, M. C., & Sun-Irminger, X. (2006, September). Assessing English language learners in mainstream classrooms. *The Reading Teacher*, 60(1), 24–34.

Leithwood, K., Seashore, K., Anderson, S. L., & Wahlstrom, K. (2004). *How leadership influences student learning: Executive summary.* Commissioned by the Wallace Foundation. New York, NY.

Levinson, E., & Surratt, J. (2004, May 10). What should superintendents know & do with technology? *Converge Magazine.* Retrieved March 15, 2007, from http://www.convergemag.com/Publications/CNVGJan99/techfromtop /techfromtop.shtm

Lieberman, A. (1995). Practices that support teacher development: Transforming conceptions of professional learning. *Phi Delta Kappan*, 76(8), 591–597.

Lightbown, P. M., & Spada, N. (1990). Focus on form and corrective feedback in communicative language teaching: Effects on second language learning. *Studies in Second Language Acquisition, 12*, 429–448.

Lord B., & Miller, B. (2000, March). *Teacher leadership: An appealing and inescapable force in school reform?* Education Development Center, Inc. Retrieved February 22, 2007, from http://www.ed.gov/inits/Math/glenn/LordMiller.doc

Loucks-Horsley, S., Hewson, P. W., Love, N., & Stiles, K. E. (1998). *Designing professional development for teachers of science and mathematics.* Thousands Oaks, CA: Corwin Press.

Lockwood, D. (1997). *Violence among middle school and high school students: Analysis and implications for prevention. National Institute of Justice Research in Brief.* Department of Justice, Washington, DC. Retrieved April 9, 2007, from ERIC database.

Marks, S. U., Schrader, C., & Levine, M. (1999). Paraeducator experiences in inclusive settings: Helping, hovering, or holding their own? *Exceptional Children, 65,* pp. 315–328.

Marland, S. P. (1971). *Education of the gifted and talented—Volume 1: Report to the Congress of the United States by the U.S. Commissioner of Education.* ERIC Document ED056243.

Marshall, M. L. (n.d.). *Examining school climate: Defining factors and emotional influences.* Center for Research on School Safety, School Climate and Classroom Management, Georgia State University. Retrieved October 30, 2006, from http://www.schoolsafety@gsu.edu

Maxwell, N. L., & Rubin, V. (2000). *High School Career Academies: A Pathway to Educational Reform in Urban Schools.* Kalamazoo, MI: W.E. Upjohn Institute for Employment Research.

Mayo Clinic. (n.d.). *Childhood obesity.* Retrieved January 2, 2007, from http://www.mayoclinic.com/health/childhood-obesity/DS00698

McEvoy, A. (2005). *Teachers who bully students: Patterns and policy implications.* Paper presented at the Hamilton Fish Institute's Persistently Safe Schools Conference, Philadelphia, PA, September 11–14.

McEvoy, A., & Welker, R. (2000). Antisocial behavior, academic failure, and school climate: A critical review. *Journal of Emotional and Behavioral Disorders, 8*(3), 130–140.

Mehta, S. (2007, February 18). More students across US logging on to online classrooms: Time restraints, jobs, yen for AP classes all factors. *Los Angeles Times.* Retrieved February 20, 2007, from http://www.boston.com/news/nation/articles/2007/02/18/more_students_across_us_logging_on_to_online_classrooms?mode=PF

Mertens, S. B., & Flowers, N. (2003). Middle school practices improve student achievement in high poverty schools. *Middle School Journal, 35*(1), 33–43.

Meyer, L. (2005). The complete curriculum: Ensuring a place for the arts in America's schools. *Art Education Policy Review, 106*(3), 35–39.

Miller, A. (2003). *Violence in U.S. public schools: 2000 school survey on crime and safety* (NCES 2004–314), revised. U.S. Department of Education, Washington, DC: National Center for Education Statistics.

Miramontes, O., Nadeau, A., & Cummins, N. (1997). *Restructuring schools for linguistic diversity.* New York: Teachers College Press.

Montecel, M. R., Cortez, J. D., & Cortez, A. (2002, April 1). *What is valuable and contributes to success in bilingual education programs.* Paper presented American Educational Research Association Annual Meeting.

National Association of Elementary School Principals (n.d.). *NAESP fact sheet on principal shortage.* Retrieved on April 6, 2007, from http://www.naesp.org/content/.oad .do?content/d=1-97&action=print

National Association for Sport and Physical Education (2006). *Shape of the nation.* Retrieved January 19, 2007, from http://www.aahperd.org/naspe/

National Association of Elementary School Principals (n. d.). *NAESP fact sheet on the principal shorage.* Retrieved January 16, 2007, from http://www.naesp.org /ContentLoad.do?contentId=1097

National Center on Educational Statistics (2001). *Dropout rates in the United States: 2000.* Retrieved January 16, 2007, from http://nces.ed.gov/pubs2002/droppub_2001 /tables/table3.asp

National Center for School Safety Checklist (1998). *Checklist of characteristics of youth who have caused school-associated violent deaths.* National School Safety Center. Retrieved September 9, 2006, from http://www.schoolsafety.us/Checklist-of -Characteristics-of-Youth-Who-Have-Caused-School-Associated-Violent-Deaths -p-7.html

National Commission on Excellence in Education (1983, April). *A nation at risk: The imperative for educational reform.* Washington, DC: U.S. Department of Education.

The National Commission on Teaching and America's Future and NCAF State Partners (2002, August 20–22). *Unraveling the "teacher shortage" problem: Teacher retention is the key.* A Symposium of the National Commission on Teaching and America's Future and NCTAF State Partners, Washington, DC.

National School Social Worker Association (2002). *NASW standards for school social work services.* Retrieved March 28, 2007, from http://www.socialworkers.org /practice/standards/NASW_SSWS.pdf

National Wellness Association (n. d.).*Definition of fitness.* Retrieved March 2, 2007, from http://nationalwellnessassociation.com/

Nelson, D. E., & Gardner, J. L. (1998). *An evaluation of the comprehensive guidance program in Utah public schools.* Salt Lake City, UT: The Utah State Office of Education.

Niles, M. D., Reynolds, A. J., & Nagasawa, M. (2006, Spring). Does early childhood intervention affect the social and emotional development of participants? *Early Childhood Research & Practice,* 8(1). University of Illinois. Retrieved January 6, 2007, from http://ecrp.uiuc.edu/v8n1/niles.html

No Child Left Behind Act. (2001). *Title IX, Part A, Section 9101(22).* Retrieved January 15, 2007, from http://www.ed.gov/policy/elsec/leg/esea02/index.html

North Carolina Department of Juvenile Justice and Delinquency Prevention (2002, May). Just what is "school violence?" *News Brief: Center for the Prevention of School Violence.* Retrieved August 2, 2006, from http://www.cpsv.org

O'Connell-Ross, P. (1993, October). *National excellence: A case for developing America's talent.* Washington, DC: U.S. Department of Education, Office of Educational Research and Development.

Office of Elementary and Secondary Education (2001) *No Child Left Behind: A Desktop Reference.* Washington, DC: U.S. Department of Education.

Ogden, C. L., Flegal, K. M., Carroll, M. D., & Johnson, C. L. (2002). Prevalence and trends in overweight among U.S. children and adolescents, 1999–2000. *Journal or the American Medical Association,* 288(14), 1728–1732.

Olweus, D. (2004). Bullying at school: Prevalence estimation, a useful evaluation design, and a new national initiative in Norway. *Association for Child Psychology and Psychiatry Occasional Papers, 23,* 5–17.

Olweus, D., Limber, S., & Mihalic, S. (1999). *Blueprints for violence prevention, book nine: Bullying prevention program.* Boulder, CO: Center for the Study and Prevention of Violence.

Palos-Tuley, B. (2003). An examination of the relationship between fine arts experiences and creative thinking, academic self-concept, and academic achievement of Hispanic students in grades 3, 4, and 5 in selected south Texas schools. (Doctoral dissertation, Texas A&M University) *Dissertation Abstracts International, 65*(1), 008A.

Parsad, B., Lewis, L., & Farris, E. (2001, June). *Teacher preparation and professional development: 2000.* U.S. Department of Education: National Center for Educational Statistics.

Pascopella, A. (2005, January). Heart of the school: The school library is as valuable as learning how to read and compute. But it's a tough sell for administrators. *The District Administrator, 41*(1), 54–55.

Peterson, K. D. (2002, Summer). At Issue: Positive or negative. *Journal of Staff Development, 23*(3), 10–15. National Staff Development Council.

Peterson, R. L., & Skiba, R. (2001). Creating school climates that prevent school violence. *The Clearing House, 74*(3), 155–163.

Pica, T. (1994). Research on negotiation: What does it reveal about second-language learning conditions, processes, and outcomes? *Language Learning, 44,* 493–527.

Pickett, A. L. (2002, Fall). Paraeducators: The evolution in their roles, responsibilities, training, and supervision. *IMPACT, 15*(2). Institute on Community Integration: Research and Training Center on Community Living.

Pink, D. H. (2005). *A whole new mind: Moving from the information age to the conceptual age.* New York: Riverhead Books.

Plank, S. (2001). *Career and technical education in the balance: An analysis of high school persistence, academic achievement, and postsecondary destinations.* St. Paul, MN: National Research Center for Career and Technical Education, University of Minnesota.

Porter, A. C., Garet, M. S., Desimone, L., Yoon, D. S., & Birman, B. F. (2000). *Does professional development change teaching practice? Results from a three-year study.* Report for U.S. Department of Education Office of the Under Secretary, DOC #2000–04.

Quality Education Data (QED). (2004). *Technology Purchasing Forecast, 2003–2004.* Denver, CO: Scholastic.

Rathburn, A., & West, J. (2004). From kindergarten through third grade: Children's beginning school experiences. (NCES 2004-007). U.S. Department of Education, National Center for Education Statistics. Washington, DC: U.S. Government Printing Office (Accessed 2006/02/21).

Reeves, D. (2000). *Accountability in action: A blueprint for learning organizations, 2nd edition.* Center for Performance Assessment, Englewood, CO: Advanced Learning Press.

Reis, S. M., & Renzulli, J. S. (2004). Current research on the social and emotional development of gifted and talented students: Good news and future possibilities. *Psychology in the schools, 41*(1), 119–130.

Reynolds, A. J., Temple, J. A., Ou, S., Robertson, D. L., Mersky, J. P., Topitzes, J. W., & Niles, M. (2006). Effects of a school-based, early childhood intervention on adult health and well being: A 20-year follow-up of low-income families. *Early Childhood Research Collaborative—Discussion Paper 102.* Retrieved March 2, 2007, from http://www.earlychildhoodrc.org/papers/DP102.pdf

Renzulli, J. (1978, November). What makes giftedness? *Phi Delta Kappan, 60*(30), 180–184, 261.

Renzulli, J., & Reis, S. M. (1997). *The schoolwide enrichment model: A comprehensive plan for educational excellence* (2nd ed.). Mansfield Center, CT: Creative Learning Press.

Robin, K. B., Frede, E. C., & Barnett, W. S. (2006). *Is more better? The effects of full-day vs. half-day preschool on early school achievement.* New Brunswick, NJ: The State University of New Jersey, National Institute for Early Education Research.

Rojewski, J. (2002). Preparing the workforce of tomorrow: A conceptual framework for career and technical education. *Journal of Vocational Education Research, 27*(1), 1–17. Retrieved June 28, 2007 from http://scholar.lib.vt.edu/ejournals/JVER/v27n1/rojewski.html

Rothenberg, D. (1995). *Full-day kindergarten programs.* Urbana, IL: ERIC Clearinghouse on Elementary and Early Childhood Education. Retrieved January 31, 2007, from ERIC database.

Rothstein, J. M. (2004). *Class and schools: Using social, economic, and educational reform to close the black-white achievement gap.* Washington, DC: Economic Policy Institute.

Roza, M., Celio, M., Harvey, J., & Wishon, S. (2003, January). *A matter of definition: Is there truly a shortage of school principals?* University of Washington: Center of Reinvention Public Education. Retrieved April 2, 2007, from http://www.crpe.org/pubs/introMatterofDefinition.shtml

Salzberg, C. L., & Morgan, J. (1995). Preparing teachers to work with paraeducators. *Teacher Education and Special Education, 18*(1), 49–55.

Schacter, J. (1999). The impact of education technology on student achievement: What the most current research has to say. *Milkin Exchange on Education Technology.* Retrieved April 23, 2007, from http://www.milkenexchange.org

Schibsted, E. (2006, December–January). Fighting for fitness: Schools battle an epidemic of childhood obesity: A problem they helped create. *Edutopia.* Retrieved June 2, 2006, from http://www.edutopia.org/magazine/dec05.php

Schmoker, M. (2006). *Results now: How we can achieve unprecedented improvements in teaching and learning.* Alexandria, VA: Association for Supervision and Curriculum Development.

Selekman, J., & Guilday, P. (2003). Identification of desired outcomes for school nursing practice. *Journal of School Nurses, 19*(6), 344–350.

Sheley, J. F., & Wright, J. D. (1998, October). High school youths, weapons, and violence: A national survey. *National Institute of Justice: Research in Brief, 81*(5), 1–7.

Shellard, E. (2002). *The informed educator: Using paraprofessionals effectively.* Arlington, VA: Educational Research Service.

Shephard, R. J. (1997). Curricular physical activity and academic performance. *Pediatric Exercise Science, 9,* 113–125.

Silverberg, M., Warner, E., Fong, M., & Goodwin, D. (2004). *National assessment of vocational education: Final report to Congress executive summary.* U.S. Department of Education: Office of the Under Secretary Policy and Program Studies Service.

Sinclair-Tarr, S., & Tarr, J. (2007). Using large-scale assessments to evaluate the effectiveness of school library programs in California. *Phi Delta Kappan, 88*(9), 710–711.

Smith, P. K., Pepler, D., & Rigby, K. (Eds.). (2004). *Bullying in schools: How successful can interventions be?* Cambridge, UK: Cambridge University Press.

Snyder, T. D., & Hoffman, C. M. (2001). *Digest of education statistics 2000.* Washington, DC: U.S. Department of Education, National Center for Education Statistics.

Spada, N., & Lightbown, P. M. (1993). Instruction and the development of questions in L2 classrooms. *Studies in Second Language Acquisition, 15*, 205–224.

Sparks, D. (2005, April). Principals serve schools as leaders of professional learning. *Results.* National Staff Development Council. Retrieved June 28, 2007, from http://www.nsdc.org/library/publications/results/res4-05spar.cfm

Steffan, N., Lance, K. C., Russell, B., & Lietzau, Z. (2004, September). *Retirement, retention, and recruitment: The future of librarianship in Colorado.* Colorado Department of Education. Retrieved November 2, 2006, from http://www.lrs.org /documents/closer_look/RRR_web.pdf

Stipek, D., Feiler, R., Daniels, D., & Milburn, S. (1995). Effects of different instructional approaches on young children's achievement and motivation. *Child Development, 66*(1), 209–223.

Strickland, D. S. (2002, February 12). Testimony given to the Senate Committee on Health, Education, Labor, and Pensions. Retrieved November 2, 2006, from http://help.senate.gov/Hearings/2002_02_12_b/Strickland.pdf

Sturm, B. (2004, October). Should we invest in paraprofessionals? *American School Board Journal, 191*(10), 34.

Swain, M. (1985). Communicative competence: Some roles of comprehensible input and comprehensible output in its development. In S. Gass & C. Madden (Eds.), *Input in second language acquisition* (pp. 235–253). Rowley, MA: Newbury House.

Swain, M. (1995). Three functions of output in second language learning. In G. Cook & B. Seidlhofer (Eds.), *Principle and practice in applied linguistics: Studies in honour of H. G. Widdowson.* New York: Oxford University Press.

Swanson, C. B. (2006). Technology Counts 2006. Tracking U.S. trends. *Education Week: The Information Edge. Using data to accelerate achievement, 25*(35), 50–53.

Symons, C. W., Cinelli, B., James, T. C., & Groff, P. (1997). Bridging student health risks and academic achievement through comprehensive school health programs. *Journal of School Health, 67*(6), 220–227.

Taras, H., Wright, S., Brennan, J., Campana, J., & Lofgren, R. (2004). Impact of School Nurse Case Management on Students with Asthma. *Journal of School Health, 74*(6), 213–220.

Thomas, W. P., & Collier, V. P. (2002). *A national study of school effectiveness for language minority students' long-term academic achievement (Final Paper No. 1.1).* Santa Cruz, CA: University of California, Center for Research on Education, Diversity, & Excellence.

Tomlinson, C. A. (1999). *The differentiated classroom: Responding to the needs of all learners.* Alexandria, VA: Association for Supervision and Curriculum Development.

Tremlow, S. W., Fonagy, P., Sacco, F. C., & Brethour, J. R., Jr. (2006). Teachers who bully students: A hidden trauma. *International Journal of Social Psychiatry, 52,* 187–198.

Tucher, P., & Tschannen-Moran, M. (2002). *School leadership in an era of accountability.* College of William and Mary: Commonwealth Educational Policy Institute. Retrieved March 22, 2007, from http://www.cepi.vcu.edu/pdf/SAELP%20Report.pdf

Upitis R., & Smithrim, K. (2003). *Learning through the arts: National assessment 1999–2002.* Final report to the Royal Conservatory. Toronto, ON: Royal Conservatory.

UCLA Center for Mental Health in Schools: Training and Technical Assistance. (2000). *Addressing barriers to learning, 5*(2). UCLA School Mental Health Project.

U.S. Census Bureau (2000, 2005, 2006). *American fact finder.* Retrieved March 31, 2007, from http://factfinder.census.gov/servlet/BasicFactsServlet?lang=en

U.S. Census Bureau (2005). *Income, poverty, and health insurance coverage in the United States: 2005.* Retrieved January 2, 2007, from http://www.uscensus.gov

U.S. Census Bureau (2005, May 17). *U.S. Census reports minority population tops 100 million.* Retrieved January 2, 2007, from http://www.uscensus.gov

U.S. Department of Health, Education, and Welfare (1971). *Education of the gifted and talented.* Washington, DC.

U.S. Department of Health and Human Services (2001). *The surgeon general's call to action to prevent and decrease overweight and obesity, 2001.* Retrieved November 23, 2006, from http://www.surgeongeneral.gov/topics/obesity/calltoaction /CalltoAction.pdf

U.S. Department of Justice, Bureau of Justice Statistics (2004). *National crime victimization survey: Unbounded data, 2004* [Computer file]. Conducted by U.S. Department of Commerce, Bureau of the Census, ICPSR04449-v1. Ann Arbor, MI: Interuniversity Consortium for Political and Social Research [producer and distributor], 2006–06–22. Retrieved June 28, 2007, from http://staging.icpsr.umich.edu/cocoon /ICPSR/STUDY/04449.xml

U.S. National Commission of Libraries and Information Science (2004). *Research Brief Winter-Threshold.* Retrieved June 28, 2007, from http://www.nclis.gov

Vaughn, K. (2002). Music and mathematics: Modest support for the oft-claimed relationship. In R. Deasy (Ed.), *Critical Links: Learning in the Arts and Student Achievement and Social Development,* pp. 96–100. Washington, DC: Arts Education Program.

Villegas, M. (2005). *Full-day kindergarten: Expanding learning opportunities. Early education. Policy brief.* San Francisco, CA: WestEd. Retrieved February 21, 2007, from ERIC database.

Villegas, M. (2003). *Leading in difficult times: Are urban school boards up to the task?* Policy Trends, pp. 1–8. San Francisco, CA: WestEd.

Walsh-Bowers, R. T. (1992). A creative drama prevention program for easing early adolescents' adjustment to school transition. *Journal of Primary Prevention, 13,* 131–147.

Waters, T., Marzano, R. J., & McNulty, B. A. (2005). *School leadership that works: From research to results.* Alexandria, VA: Association for Supervision and Curriculum Development.

Wedl, R. J. (2005, July). Response to intervention: An alternative to traditional eligibility criteria for students with disabilities. Education Evolving: Center for Policy Studies and Hamline University. Retrieved June 28, 2007, from http://educationevolving .org/pdf/Response_to_Intervention.pdf

Wentzel, K. R. (1997). Student motivation in middle school: The role of perceived pedagogical caring. Journal of Educational Psychology, 89, 411–419.

Westberg, K. L., Archambault, F. X., Dobyns, S. M., & Salvan, T. J. (1993, Winter). The
classroom practices observation study. Journal for the Education of the Gifted, 16(2),
120–146.

WestEd (2003). Leadership development: Enhancing the role of teachers. R&D Alert,
4(3), 1–9.

Wheatley, M. (1992). Leadership and the new science: Learning about organization
from an orderly universe. San Francisco: Berrett-Koehler.

Wikipedia. (n.d.). Meta-analysis. Retrieved June 28, 2007, from http://en.wikipedia
.org/wiki/Meta-analysis

Wilkins, J.L.M., Graham, G., & Parker, S. (2003). Time in the arts and physical education and school achievement. Journal of Curriculum Studies, 35(6), 721–734.

Willard, N. E. (2005). A parent's guide to cyberbullying and cyberthreats. Center for
Safe and Responsible Internet Use. Retrieved March 2, 2007, from http://www
.cyberbully.org/docs/cbctparents.pdf

Whitaker, K. (2001). Where are the principal candidates? Perceptions of superintendents. NASSP Bulletin, 85, 82. Washington DC: Sage. Retrieved May 7, 2007, from
http://www.sagepublications.com/

Wolak, J., Mitchell, K., & Finkelhor, D. (2006). Online victimization of youth: Five years
later. National Center for Missing & Exploited Children. Retrieved March 2, 2007,
from http://www.missingkids.com/

Woodworth, K. R., Gallagher, H. A., Guha, R., Campbell, A. Z., Lopez-Torkos, A. M., &
Kim, D. (2007). An unfinished canvas. Arts education in California: Taking stock of
policies and practices. Summary Report. Menlo Park, CA: SRI International.

Woolls, B. (2004). The school library media manager, 3rd ed. Westport, CT: Libraries
Unlimited.

Word, E., Johnston, J., Bain, H. P., & Fulton, B. D. (1990). The state of Tennessee's stu-
dent/teacher achievement ratio project. Final summary report, 1985–1990. Tennessee
State Department of Education.

Wright, S. P., Horn, S. P., & Sanders, W. L. (1997). Teacher and classroom context effects on student achievement: Implications for teacher evaluation. Journal of Personnel Evaluation in Education, 11, 57–67.

ABOUT THE AUTHORS

Sandra Watkins is associate professor of Educational Leadership at Western Illinois University. Before joining the faculty at Western Illinois University, Sandra served public schools as a teacher, guidance director, guidance coordinator, school psychologist, coordinator of gifted programs, elementary and middle school principal, assistant superintendent, and associate superintendent. The majority of her work has centered on district and school improvement. She has extensive experience as a turnaround leader at both the school and district levels. She has worked with schools and districts across the country on school- and district-level improvement challenges. In addition, she has taught graduate classes at the University of North Carolina–Greensboro, Furman University, Creighton University, and the University of New Hampshire.

Watkins has authored publications that focus on the importance of vision, mission, and core values in schools and districts, professional development, school boards, accountability for results, as well as videos that focus on data-driven decision making, the importance of vision, and the identification of underachieving gifted and talented students. She is an active national presenter at the American Association of School Administrators, the Illinois School Board Association, the National School Boards Association, the National Council for Professor of Educational Administration, and the National Rural Educators Association.

Donna McCaw teaches graduate and doctoral coursework in educational leadership at Western Illinois University in Macomb. The daughter of two uneducated but highly intelligent parents—who instilled in her a drive to "be part of the solution," Dr. McCaw received her doctorate in curriculum and instruction from Illinois State University. She has a M.A. in counseling, a M.S.Ed., and a B.S. in speech and language pathology. Before teaching at the university, Dr. McCaw served as an elementary school principal, director of curriculum, elementary school counselor, and speech pathologist. She has worked extensively for more than 30 years with schools and districts on continuous improvement, professional development, and literacy. She is married to Mark, her bestest friend. They have one daughter, Sara; one son-in-law, Larry; and one chocolate lab granddog, Reilly.